Hiking the Florida Trail

WILD FLORIDA

UNIVERSITY PRESS OF FLORIDA

Florida A&M University, Tallahassee
Florida Atlantic University, Boca Raton
Florida Gulf Coast University, Ft. Myers
Florida International University, Miami
Florida State University, Tallahassee
New College of Florida, Sarasota
University of Central Florida, Orlando
University of Florida, Gainesville
University of North Florida, Jacksonville
University of South Florida, Tampa
University of West Florida, Pensacola

Hiking the Florida Trail

1,100 Miles, 78 Days, Two Pairs of Boots,
and One Heck of an Adventure

Johnny Molloy

Foreword by M. Timothy O'Keefe

University Press of Florida
Gainesville/Tallahassee/Tampa/Boca Raton
Pensacola/Orlando/Miami/Jacksonville/Ft. Myers/Sarasota

WILD FLORIDA

edited by M. Timothy O'Keefe

Books in this series are written for the many people who visit and/or move to Florida to participate in our remarkable outdoors, an environment rich in birds, animals, and activities, many exclusive to this state. Books in the series will offer readers a variety of formats: Natural history guides, historical outdoor guides, guides to some of Florida's most popular pastimes and activities, and memoirs of outdoors folk and their unique lifestyles.

30 Eco-trips in Florida: The Best Nature Excursions and How to Reduce Your Impact on the Environment, by Holly Ambrose (2005)

A Hiker's Guide to the Sunshine State, by Sandra Friend (2005)

Fishing Florida's Flats: A Guide to Bonefish, Tarpon, Permit, and Much More, by Jan S. Maizler (2007)

50 Great Walks in Florida, by Lucy Beebe Tobias (2008)

Hiking the Florida Trail, by Johnny Molloy (2008)

Copyright 2008 by Johnny Molloy
Printed in the United States of America on acid-free paper

13 12 11 10 09 08   6 5 4 3 2 1

Library of Congress Cataloging-in-Publication Data
Molloy, Johnny, 1961–
Hiking the Florida trail: 1,100 miles, 78 days, two pairs of boots,
and one heck of an adventure/Johnny Molloy; foreword by
M. Timothy O'Keefe.
p. cm.—(Wild Florida)
ISBN 978-0-8130-3195-8 (pbk.: alk. paper)
1. Florida Trail (Fla.)—Guidebooks. 2. Hiking—Florida—
Guidebooks. 3. Trails—Florida—Guidebooks. 4. Florida—
Guidebooks. I. Title.
GV199.42.F6M648 2008
796.5109759—dc22   2007028878

The University Press of Florida is the scholarly publishing
agency for the State University System of Florida, comprising
Florida A&M University, Florida Atlantic University, Florida
Gulf Coast University, Florida International University, Florida
State University, University of Central Florida, University of
Florida, University of North Florida, University of South Florida,
and University of West Florida.

University Press of Florida
15 Northwest 15th Street
Gainesville, FL 32611-2079
http://www.upf.com

Contents

Foreword

The University Press of Florida celebrates the essential natural qualities of Florida, its environment, its creatures, and its people through the broad-ranging series Wild Florida.

Hiking the Florida Trail by veteran hiker Johnny Molloy illustrates the wide-ranging approach to UPF's commitment to exploring, appreciating, and protecting our Wild Florida.

With Florida ranked as one of the most populous states and hundreds of thousands more people moving here every year, it seems impossible that truly wild places can remain anywhere in such a densely inhabited region. Yet in spite of the tremendous influx of people wanting to enjoy the Sunshine State's warm climate and active outdoor lifestyle, significant sections of the original, natural Florida do still endure.

In fact, the amount of land and shoreline Florida has set aside for preservation surprises many people, especially first-time visitors and newly arrived residents. As this is written, Florida terrain is protected by three national forests, 11 national parks, 157 state parks, and 28 national wildlife refuges. In addition, individual counties have designated their own protected public lands, providing for pristine rivers and sheltered coastline. There is indeed a good deal of Florida that has not been paved over or disturbed by development; and it never will be.

In *Hiking the Florida Trail*, Johnny Molloy leads you through many of the state's most pristine areas. Starting at the Big Cypress trailhead deep in the Everglades and ending in the western Panhandle at the Florida-Alabama border, he energetically shares the sights, sounds, smells, and hardships of walking one of only eight national scenic trails in the United States.

It's a journey that offers something for all of us. Most of us may never walk the entire Florida Trail, but we can take advantage of how its convenient trailheads near major roadways place numerous segments of the trail within an hour's drive of most residents and even the major tourist destinations. Short loop hikes of only a few miles are available in many state parks, making ideal family outings with the added zest of camping, either in primitive conditions or with electricity and running water.

Since much of the Florida Trail is still in private ownership, long distance hikers will need to join the Florida Trail Association (www. floridatrail.org) in Gainesville. Only FTA members enjoy access to the entire route, plus FTA has the most detailed set of hiking maps available. Those maps are as essential as water and bug spray.

On his three-month journey through America's only subtropical landscape, Johnny Molloy loses fifteen pounds and requires two sets of hiking shoes, discarding his first pair of low-top lightweights after sixty days and eight hundred miles (or "ten cents per mile . . . well worth it," he notes). Indeed, shoes worn on the Florida Trail do often endure more extreme conditions than may be encountered on some other trails. Trails outside Florida may appear tougher because they are known for their numerous ups and downs, yet such terrain is more likely to wear out the hiker than the boots.

In Florida, water and mud are constant trail companions. Johnny's first step plunges him into water as he begins his trek northward, following the FT's bright orange blazes through tall, thick sawgrass bordering a bald cypress swamp. It doesn't seem especially noteworthy, but if you've ever walked in soft sand at the edge of the waves, you know how tiring that can be. Now imagine doing this with a forty-two-pound backpack while pushing doggedly against an oncoming cold front. Trail slogging (or sloshing), you might call it.

Yes, some sections of the trail can be tough. However, as those of us who have walked parts of it know, the new experiences and realizations are worth it. At the end, Johnny admits he was "more awestruck" by the beauty of Florida's mosaic of landscapes than he ever expected to be. And then there are the special, unforgettable moments: "Just as we retired, the moon rose between the pines, forcing me to cover my eyes with a bandana tied around my head. . . . The frogs were staging an amphibian musical all around us, drowning out even the usual evening bugs. They croaked in time, rising to a crescendo, then fell off, then rose again. . . . It was a much richer lullaby than those sleep tapes people play by their bed, mimicking ocean waves and the like. This was the real thing."

This book is the real thing, too. Shoes tied? Water bottles ready? Let's go walking in the Florida wilderness.

M. Timothy O'Keefe
Series Editor

Let It Rip!

My very first step went into water. Brash gusts of wind forced their way south, wildly blowing my wide-brimmed hat about, and competed with my sloshing shoes for audio supremacy. The wet trail sliced through sawgrass bordered with bald cypress trees. Minnows darted in the crystalline water before my moving feet, as I negotiated submerged potholes of white rock. I pushed north over what was once known as Old Sawmill Road, a decades-abandoned plank-lined track, now left to hikers such as myself, making our way on the Florida Trail, from its modest, inauspicious, and hard-to-find beginning in the Big Cypress National Preserve to the trail's northern terminus in the Florida Panhandle. I had thought about this adventure—hiking the Florida Trail—for years. Now that it had nearly come to fruition, I was weary of thinking about it, weary of talking about it, weary of planning for it and was simply ready to walk.

Numerically speaking, I was a forty-four-year-old, 196-pound man. A too-heavy forty-two-pound pack rested on my shoulders. It would ride there for 1,100 miles to the Florida Trail's conclusion. I was thinking about how good luck had already befallen me. After arriving at the Big Cypress trailhead, I had hurriedly got out of the Jeep with my gear, ready to go. My Minnesota friends John and Barb Haapala were sending me off and taking the care of my Jeep while I was gone. We were snapping pictures at the remote trailhead when up drove some tourists from Wisconsin. They pulled over and got out in the fashion tourists do, stopping to see whatever it might be that someone else has stopped to see.

I was tying and retying my shoes, trying to get it right, irritated at nothing in particular, just ready to go. A slender older woman walked up and gently asked: "Did someone drop this?" I looked up to find my wallet in her hand! It was full of money, identification, bank cards, and more—all of which I would certainly need in order to accomplish my journey.

I thanked her kindly and stowed the wallet in my pack. "I hope you don't drop anything else along the way," said John in his practical way and thick North Country accent. I thanked John and Barb for dropping me off. They took one last picture, then I turned, taking that first step, falling into rhythmic alternating steps, pushing one foot in front of the other through the water, swamp slogging.

Movement at my feet—a snake! I danced a spirited jig, legs contorting in fast motion, successfully avoiding the equally shocked serpent, which slithered into the sawgrass. How ironic! The most common comment from well wishers upon hearing about my planned Florida Trail hike had been: "Watch out for the snakes and alligators." Maybe they were onto something. Here was the first surprise of the journey, not five minutes into it. But I was ready for anything, even a slithering snake in the trail. My motto for this adventure was: "Let it rip!" I was ready for the best laid plans to meet unforeseen circumstances, and a snake was not exactly unforeseen.

The second surprise was already in motion, though not as rapid as the snake. The powering winds blowing in my ears were the leading edge of a cold front, pushing frosty air into the southernmost reaches of Florida. Tonight would be a cold one. But I didn't care about heat or cold; I was excited to be under way. My start date was three weeks removed from the winter solstice, and the hours of light—already longer than back home in East Tennessee—were growing longer.

The Big Cypress scenery was as portrayed in the pictures of famous South Florida photographer Clyde Butcher. Tall groups of cypress, collectively known as domes, and pine stands, where the ground was somewhat higher and drier, broke an expansive sawgrass plain. The domes and stands resembled hills of brown and green over which floated puffy white clouds in an impossibly blue sky. Along the trail

They took one last picture, then I turned around, taking that first step.

dwarf pond cypress rose from the sawgrass and stretched their stiff, contorted limbs like props for a scary movie.

By 1:45 p.m., I had completed my first mile. Only 1,099 more to go. Mud splayed onto my legs with each step, reflecting the terrain, which was not quite land and not quite water, but quite certainly the Big Cypress. I was getting used to it. We humans are the most adaptable creatures on the planet. Whatever the stimuli may be, whether we are living a billionaire's life in South Beach or a prisoner's life in Starke, we simply get used to it.

I began to imagine my destination—Frog Hammock—as the pine islands in the distance. Of course Frog Hammock, a dry island in this sea of sawgrass, was a little farther than I thought. An axiom of self-propelled wilderness travel is that you have rarely gone as far as you think you have. Eventually, also known as three miles, the Florida Trail led into the thick woods of lightly used Frog Hammock. The increase in elevation amounted to scarcely a foot, but that was high and dry enough for a thru-hiking backpacker to throw up a camp. In wet years, Frog Hammock would be fit only for a frog.

I walked to the center of the woodland, dropping my pack against a tree. A fire ring made of broken cinder blocks marked the spot. A pump well, now just a corroded worthless edifice, stood in the distance. Frog Hammock had seen busier days. Other rusty relics revealed the area to have been hunt camp of some sort at one time. An old stove, a tank, and creaky box springs hinted at the past.

The gusty wind pounded into the dense woods, occasionally penetrating my little island in the Big Cypress. The broken pump well necessitated a short search for water, which I found in a limestone solution hole nearby. A solution hole is a pocket where water gathers in the limestone rock bed that underlies South Florida, an ever so slightly tilted layer of stone sloping so as to allow water to flow southward from Central Florida through the Big Cypress and onward through the Everglades to the Gulf of Mexico.

The water in the solution hole was alive with swimming critters, and I took this as a good sign, for poisonous water would harbor no aquatic life. Of course, to drink it, you had to be willing to drink a few of the critters along with the welcome water. Back at camp, I started a campfire to make a little coffee. Unloading the pack to find coffee makings, I found an extra toothbrush but no coffee filters. The best laid plans . . . Part of letting it rip was to roll with the punches. I simply made "camp coffee," letting the grounds steep in the aluminum pot I used to heat water over the fire. I could save time by using both toothbrushes at once.

Creeping cold rolled into the inevitable dark, settling like fog. I dried my hiking socks on some sticks propped before the flames. Two pairs would be required to keep my feet warm that night, but I burned a hole in one sock during the drying process. A pale, pocked full moon rose over the adjacent pines. I scooted a little closer to the fire, following the progress of the white orb as it crossed the sky, obscuring all but the brightest of stars.

In the distance an owl hooted. This was as I had imagined it to be. The Florida Trail end-to-end hike was on.

2

Firemen of the Holy Lands

The moon was still up, setting in a morning sky. A low in the thirties chilled the swamp water, which in turn numbed my feet. I pushed forward on the watery track amid dwarf cypress. Frog Hammock fell behind me. Sometimes the path led through knee-deep water even in the domes of tall cypress. Deep or shallow, the water made for slow passage. After an indeterminate time of slogging, I could see land ahead. Walking on the land would warm my feet and speed my progress. The palms and pines and tropical hardwoods welcomed me.

But soon things went wrong. Numerous trees had fallen across this portion of the Florida Trail (FT), especially the brushlike wax myrtle. The hurricanes of the previous year had wreaked disorder upon the exposed hammocks of the Big Cypress. Here the trail was officially closed, and I soon found out why. Like America's most famous footpath, the Appalachian Trail, the FT is blazed, which means rectangular paint markings on trees demarcate the trail. The blazes of the FT are orange, reflecting one of the state's claims to fame. While hiking the FT, you follow the orange blazes.

Back in the early 1960s a man from Miami named Jim Kern returned to his home state after hiking the Appalachian Trail, with the idea of creating a long distance hiking path in the Sunshine State. He founded something called the Florida Trail Association, and in 1966 he painted the first orange blaze marking the Florida Trail, in the Ocala National Forest near Clearwater Lake. With the help of a few thousand friends, his vision of a 500-mile hiking path has been extended to over 1,000 miles of protected trail corridor, and it is still growing.

Jim might not be too happy with the current state of the trail in the Big Cypress, since not only were many of the blazed trees down, but other fallen trees obscured the trail entirely. Hikers before me, attempting to find the correct path, had made tracks to nowhere. I followed some, dead-ending in thickets. Back and forth I went, crawling, climbing, and clambering over, under, and around the vegetation, fighting against limbs that snapped back and vines that ensnared my legs. At one point I found myself on my knees, right foot wrapped in a vine, backpack stuck on a limb, brush pushing down the neck of my shirt, and with a spider web in my face. How did I get there? More important, how was I going to get out? Orange blazes were not to be found. In less than twenty-four hours, this expedition was getting more and more adventurous.

I tore from the bonds and proceeded into the perceived point of least resistance, crawling over crackling leaves and limbs. After more wrangling, the hammock opened to a cypress dome. The deep water was easier to negotiate than the junglesque hammock. After that tangled land walk where progress was measured in yards per hour instead of miles per hour, I now loved swamp slogging. Sloshing east, then north, then west, I finally found an orange blaze on a cypress tree. The trail!

My good fortune was short-lived. The woods closed up into thickets, eventually leading to more swamp, where bromeliads cloaked the cypress trees. Moving water, the deepest yet, indicated that this was Roberts Strand, a year-round channel. I crossed the thigh-high watercourse and proceeded into a cypress-sawgrass plain. The track picked up an old tram road, heading due west, then north. The biting winter wind was stronger in the open, but this, too, was better than battling through tree tangles.

The blow also pushed car and truck noise south from US Highway 41. The sounds meant that the Big Cypress Oasis Visitor Center on US 41 was near. The five-mile stretch from Frog Hammock to Oasis ended in a pure mud-slopping open section only a hog would love. The visitor center was full of cars and tourists milling in the sun, collectively surprised at the South Florida chill. I sat in the warming rays with mud-clogged boots, splotches of dried muck sprayed on my red-scratched legs. While sitting in the parking lot, I noticed that my lightweight sleeping air mattress had come off during the tussle in the fallen trees, leaving me with less comfortable sleeping options.

I waited for two friends, Hans Hollmann and Jeff Cochran, the fabulous firemen from Miramar. They had agreed to hike the FT for the thirty-mile stretch from US 41 to Interstate 75. Shortly they pulled up, jumping out with clean clothes and big smiles. Then came the jokes about my muddy and scratched-up self and questions about leading them into the "Swamp of No Return." Nervous twitter in their laughs revealed concern. My bedraggled lower half clearly bespoke the challenges of the Big Cypress.

The three of us took off, leaving the visitor center behind, heading into the north wind under bright blue skies. They walked with trepidation, waiting for the first bog. But for a while all we found were a few mudholes. The FT traveled through mostly pinelands broken by short stretches of cypress flats. The packs settled onto their backs as Hans and Jeff recalled previous backpacking trips. It had been a while for both of them. The three of us had been on canoeing trips together in the past. That was how we had met. A few years back I had been rewriting *A Canoeing and Kayaking Guide to Florida* when Hans had contacted me over the Internet. He was interested in paddling the Everglades, about which I had also written a book. I asked him about his favorite streams in South Florida. He was a Peace River aficionado and offered to guide me down the river, along with Jeff. We floated the river, camping out for two nights, and had a great time. The two of them had met while working fire and rescue for the South Florida city of Miramar.

Hans changed my view of South Floridians. Despite my extensive visits to the area, I imagined all South Floridians living a fast-paced racy lifestyle with few restraints. But forty-something Hans was a hardworking family man with the good family to go along with it. Hans was born in Puerto Rico to German immigrant parents, who moved to Florida when he was six. He had become a fireman in his late teens and returned to the job after a couple of youthful exploratory stints elsewhere.

Hans bounced ahead with his pack, then abruptly stopped. The trail led directly into water. I plunged in without hesitation, having already traversed miles like this; the two firemen realized this was the moment of truth. Jeff gingerly skirted the edge while Hans plowed in. Soon, both of them were up to their knees. I looked back and laughed at their Big Cypress Swamp initiation. Little did they know just how many miles they were going to walk through water.

Seven Mile Camp, our destination, was actually a little short of seven miles from the visitor center, in dry pineland with patches of low palmetto scrub. A sign marked the actual campsite. We picked a

Seven Mile Camp, our destination, was in dry pineland with patches of low palmetto scrub. A sign marked the actual camp.

spot and then collected our camp water from a nearby cypress dome, wading toward its center until we hit a deep spot.

Jeff and Hans set up their tents while I got the fire going. The chill was returning with the falling sun. We ate dinner by the glow of greater Miami. Later the moon rose, bathing Seven Mile Camp in pale white light. Tall pines silhouetted the lunar glow. By 9:00 p.m. the temperature had dropped into the 40s, and it would go down more before dawn. I slept in a tightly cinched bag by the fire, periodically feeding it during the night.

The sun rose slowly over frosty Seven Mile Camp. This was January 16, my third day on the FT. Jeff and Hans stirred, coming to the fire heavy lidded and heavily clad. I already had a little coffee in my system. Soon we were northbound, with the sun angling onto our backs and the wind in our faces as we wound primarily through pineland. The trailbed grew fainter beyond Seven Mile Camp. Forest debris was on and around the trail. Most hikers head to Seven Mile Camp and then backtrack to US 41. Ahead, we often had to stop and look for the orange blazes. Having three pairs of eyes paid off, as we could scan the landscape more efficiently for orange rectangles painted on trees.

The problem was we also had to look down for limestone potholes in the trailbed. Jeff jokingly called some sections of trail the "Holy Lands" as they were full of holes that could turn or break an ankle with one misstep. "This section is a steeplechase," Hans said. "The fallen trees are the hurdles and the swamps are the water traps." The day had warmed by the time we reached Ten Mile Camp, marked with a sign. We pressed on, entering more and more wet sawgrass prairies with dwarf pond cypress. Occasional pine islands allowed our shoes to drain. On one island we found a large pile of bear scat, full of acorns. At 750,000 acres, the Big Cypress is more than big enough for a few bears to roam. I bet this bear knew the location of every live oak for miles. Live oaks were the source of these acorns. Aboriginal Floridians also prized acorns.

Jeff was bringing up the rear, ultra-concerned about twisting his ankle despite having trekking poles that aided his balance. I looked up from the pocked limestone enough to keep on the right track. We curved around a tall sawgrass prairie amid the dwarf pond cypress. The deep green of the head-high sawgrass contrasted with the ghoulish gray and white of the winter cypress world. But winter is the only time to hike the Florida Trail comfortably from end to end. The warmer times of year bring rain, more bugs, and more heat. And perhaps a hurricane. The best way to hike the FT is from south to north, to keep the winter and early spring sun at your back. This gives you the opportunity to follow spring as it heads north, too.

It was almost hot by the time we reached Thirteen Mile Camp, actually located seventeen miles from the Oasis Visitor Center on US 41. Toppled victims of recent hurricanes spread across the island of pine, palm, and live oaks. We fought our way to the campsite, just a small grassy area with a defunct pump well standing in its center, and happily shed our packs to enjoy the shade. The ten-mile day had worn on my compadres and on me. No matter how much you train, no substitute exists for actually backpacking. Furthermore, the very nature of swamp slogging is quite exhausting. You take a step forward into mud. Your foot sinks. You then push off with the same foot, digging in deeper, getting only limited leverage to move forward as your foot sinks. The other foot moves forward and lands in the mud and sinks. Repeat the process over and over. You do twice the work with half the results of hiking on dry ground. But what would the Big Cypress Swamp be without some mud walking? Undisturbed, the waters of the swamp were quite clear. Our footsteps were what muddied the water.

My pack was too heavy, with excess food and a few other experimental items sure to fall by the wayside. One valuable item was a bag of fatwood, the inner part of an aged pine tree trunk. Barb and John had given it to me. This wood was particularly rich in resins and made superlative fire starter. I used the fatwood to start a little conflagration at Thirteen Mile Camp, cooking sausages over the fire to go along with rice. Jeff and Hans searched their packs for food that would rid them of weight to carry, eating the heaviest fare. We joked about who was the fool with the heaviest pack.

Campfire camaraderie is one of the greatest joys of sharing outdoor adventures. In the evening, after sharing the toils of breaking camp, hiking, and making camp, the bonds built are revealed as fellow campers relax, recounting the day's events and letting the conversation go wherever it may lead. No cell phones ring, and you have no television, no traffic—no distractions; nothing but the natural world around, which is itself relaxing.

The next morning wild turkeys gobbled in the distance as I retrieved water from a nearby cypress dome. Wildlife was all around us, and we saw evidence of its presence, but our swamp slogging and sloshing and talking ran everything off before we arrived. Deer tracks continually crossed the FT. I couldn't help but wonder if a panther lurked in the distance, unseen, for where deer roam, the Florida panther follows. Deer are its preferred fare. Nature operates with brutal efficiency. The weakest deer are the ones that get taken—the young, the old, the sick or lame. This way the strongest survive, strengthening the gene pool and perpetuating the species.

Panthers also eat armadillos, wild hogs, raccoons, waterfowl, small alligators, and rabbits. The panther needs remoteness, too, and the Big Cypress has plenty of that. Yet the Big Cypress is but part of the greater protected area where one of our nation's rarest mammals lives. Having once ranged throughout much of the South, the panther persisted only in the wildlands of South Florida, hence the use of the name Florida panther. Only one hundred or so are left, and given the habitat losses, that may be the sustainable population, with little opportunity for expansion unless they become accustomed to living near people, as coyotes do. Wildlife managers have introduced panthers from Texas to expand the Florida panther gene pool.

The trail continued to seek the margins between the pine and cypress, where the terrain was open, avoiding trees and brush, and heading through sawgrass, which was sporadically underwater. This trail route was easy to lay out and maintain. Pine islands were often overgrown with saw palmetto and other trees, requiring routine cutting; if trees were not kept trimmed, the trail would soon become hard to follow. The cypress trees in the sawgrass plains and the thick domes had survived the hurricane damage quite well, with their fi-brous trunks, squat limbs, and small leaves. However, in island ham-mocks with leaf-heavy hardwoods it looked as if—well, as if a hur-ricane had been through. Still, the damage consisted of nothing more than downed trees, in contrast to the devastation in populated areas with their preponderance of man's works struck down. Disasters hap-pen only where people live. A hurricane toppling trees in the Big Cypress was the natural order of things.

Man's works were a long way from the heart of the Big Cypress. Thirteen Mile Camp is perhaps the most isolated, least accessible spot in South Florida; no one lived anywhere nearby, and the greater area only ever had but a small number of Indians, the Miccosuke and the Seminole. After leaving camp the next morning, Hans and Jeff were confident, having "gotten their feet wet" with the swamp slogging and also having fewer miles to travel. We pushed hard in the slight morning chill, taking a break in the shade of a palm after an hour and a half. It was just a matter of putting in the time that day.

We soon left the pines for good, entering full-blown flooded cy-press prairie. Our pace dwindled to just over a mile an hour. The sun's heat drifted over the prairie and stopping places were nonexistent, as the low-slung trees and watery plain offered nowhere to pause. The landscape took on a sameness, as if we were going in circles. Hans was bringing up the rear now, taking short rest breaks by leaning over and placing his hands on his knees to change the weight distribution of his pack. I call this "knee dropping"; exhausted backpackers com-monly do it. The deeper cypress domes offered some shade, and the waters rose to our knees, cooling our legs.

We came upon a barbed wire fence, a relic from who knows when, strung by who knows whom, herding who knows what. It was very out of place in this middle-of-nowhere. Before us stretched a vast tri-chrome world—winter blue sky, the white pond cypress domes of varied elevation, and the tannish green of the waters from which the cypress grew and through which we walked. Water levels vary here throughout the year, for South Florida has a wet season and a dry season. Winter and early spring mark the dry season, when rainfall

Stopping places were nonexistent, as the low-slung trees and watery plain offered nowhere to pause.

was scant, following the summer and fall bouts of giant cloudbursts and bigger hurricanes. During the rainy times, wetlands like the Big Cypress recharge, then slowly drain off during the dry season. We were walking through last fall's hurricane rains.

The green island of Oak Hill Camp finally came into view. The three of us tunneled through the downed trees to a small campsite at the center, at the height of the island. Someone with imagination had dubbed it a hill. Live oaks towered overhead and our world closed as if we had entered a storm shelter in the great plains of Kansas. Our lunch respite was welcome. Hans looked as if he could camp there. But it was shortly time to go again; when you are long distance hiking, the time to go often comes quickly. We left that darkened world of Oak Hill Camp, traversing dwarf pond cypress expanses, following "the ribbon of mud," as Hans called it. Since he was bringing up the rear, he always walked through a freshly stirred-up mud. The front man dropped his feet into clear water.

I got ahead of the two firemen, sloshing in the sunshine. Despite my noise a hawk landed but fifteen feet distant, on a low cypress limb. Its eyes radiated clarity and purpose. Its feathery coat was a glorious mosaic of tawny shades, a robe fit for the royals of an outdoor empire. The bird could fly quietly and purposefully, scanning the country below for the slightest movement of prey, swooping down to pick off a field mouse or some other creature. It had enough of me and flew to a tree farther away, calling out to all within earshot that the Big Cypress was its special domain. And so it was. Or was that bird that flew over the swamp with such grace laughing at us mortals, tromping through the muck with the precision of a bulldozer?

I waited for the two South Floridians at a confusing point where the trail hit an open watery plain, near sparsely scattered cypress. The wading was deep here, and the white limestone showed through the swamp water. Hans commented on the underwater cosmos, an aquatic miniworld of life and death where little fish can rule their flooded kingdom.

The FT neared a few wooded islands, which were too damp and too dense for stopping. They were just a tease for weary walkers. The long day was getting longer. What had looked like a four-hour jaunt was turning into a nine-hour marathon. I plowed on, escaping the grumbles of my comrades. Considerably later a large green palm-covered island showed in the distance. Surely that must be Ivy Camp, our intended destination. But no, the trail was not going near the island, instead staying in the wet cypress where no potential campsite was to be seen. A tiny green speck finally appeared in the gray distance. It was only a tenth the size of the previous island—surely that wasn't the campsite? Indeed, the FT began angling toward the small island. Camp! A sign indicated confirmed this as our destination, Ivy Camp. The small but mostly open island was ringed in cypress. Jeff and Hans labored in, muttering about never doing this segment of the FT again, thank you.

My shoes were filled with swamp debris, so I walked out to the deepest nearby dome and washed them out. The volume of sand and sludge was unbelievable. Hans declared he had enough sand in his shoes to form a small beach.

"Staying focused on the uneven footing—it wore me out," said Jeff.

"The actual slogging strained my leg muscles," added Hans, as we took inventory of our aches and pains. "I knew I was going to make it. I just had to take a lot of breaks to do it."

"The ferns and bromeliads and sawgrass landscape are what make hiking in the Big Cypress the most unique hiking in the lower forty-eight," I said, trying to be upbeat about the hike.

Jeff wasn't buying. "This island is my favorite part so far," he concluded. The comments continued as the afternoon wind died. Fireflies came on at dusk, as did the mosquitoes. Hans broke out his bug jacket, literally a jacket made of bug netting. Jeff and I applied bug dope and put on clothes to ward off the pesky insects. The challenges weren't over yet. Overnight, a storm hit. I was ready, however, with my ultralight tarp/poncho. It weighs five ounces and, at four by eight feet, provides about thirty square feet of room. Beneath it I hung my ultralight bug netting, also weighing five ounces. The hot evening made the netting stuffy, but the bugs at Ivy Camp mandated it. Hans and Jeff were secure in their tents. The storm hit at around 4:30 in the morning, testing the thin tarp for all it was worth. The setup survived the winds, which were still howling as I arose. Scudding clouds pushed south overhead while breaking the dark, damp camp. The swamp slogging continued along mostly submerged trail for another two miles, and then pine islands, palm islands, and what passed for dry ground afforded us easier passage.

A flock of white ibis nested in the trees of a deep cypress dome ahead. I crept slowly forward, as quietly as I could when walking through water. They began to move uneasily, then suddenly, as one, whooshed overhead squawking and flapping to a more secure locale.

The FT joined an ultrawide buggy road just before reaching I-75. The roar of cars, trucks, and buses was immense and ear-splitting after days of nothing but natural sounds. The three of us soon reached the visitor center and it was time to part ways. I thanked my firefighting buddies for coming along and helping me as they did, sharing friendship, encouragement, and a few swamps. I passed on under the interstate and continued on the Florida Trail, heading into untrod territory, now alone. What lay ahead?

3

You Never Know Who's Inside the Tent Next Door

The Florida Trail began to trace old Nobles Road, a raised track heading north through the Big Cypress. A canal lay left of the trail, created when fill was taken to make the road. Alligators hung out along the waterway, numbering more than I would see during the rest of the trip. I stopped at a convenient gator-less spot beside the canal and rinsed out my shoes and socks. They were once again filled with swamp muck and sand that rubbed my feet raw. It would be a while before I could walk with dry shoes and socks, but this was a start. The gloomy and cool Big Cypress was all my own. Save for the interstate rest stop, I had not seen a soul beyond our own party since back near US 41. And we think of South Florida as being overrun with people. It depends on where you go.

The roar of I-75 dimmed as I melded deeper into the backcountry. Palms grew in the margin between the canal and the trail. Occasional bridges and remnants of bridges spanned the canal to my left. Nobles Road provided a dry swift track and a welcome change for my feet. The landscape, a bit drier than in the lower Big Cypress, was also the site of ongoing exotic plant extermination. Brazilian pepper trees had sprung up in thickets, crowding out native species. I could see the results of efforts to cut them down and clear them out, leaving native species to repopulate. I made fast miles and came upon the old Nobles homesite and airstrip, now just an area of tall grass broken by a few metal relics. A lone broken street lamp marked the airstrip building, leaving a long stretch of grass with nowhere to fly. I rejected the

Nobles backcountry site, as the early afternoon wind was buffeting the site's position beside the old airstrip. Instead, I headed down the trail a few hundred yards for a copse of wide-spreading live oaks with a thick understory of palms and brush that defeated the breezes, leaving me a calm, dry locale. The clouds broke up during the afternoon, and I dried my gear in the sun. Yellow and black butterflies chased each other playfully around the campsite. That night I continued drying my shoes and socks around the fire, this time without incident.

In the morning, while breaking camp, I had the nagging notion of having forgotten something. What was missing? Then I realized: no keys! You don't need keys to lock your campsite door, or to start your feet up. I had no keys with me at all. John and Barb were in charge of the Jeep, and I was not going home to Johnson City, Tennessee, for a long while. I didn't need any keys. Ha! What a relief to be free from carrying those metal contraptions we use and chase around on a daily basis. Think of the aggregate minutes of your life you have spent looking for keys. It was one more freeing thing about the long distance hike.

Free to think about living in a keyless world and free on this easier section not to pay such close attention to every step on the trail, I was also free to make a bungle. My right foot caught a limb extending onto the trail, providing a crisp illustration of motion versus inertia. Momentum propelled the backpack forward, which propelled my head forward onto the dew-covered cold ground. I smashed my hands down first and rolled over a couple of times. Ironic it certainly was, after slogging through dozens of miles of swamps, that I would take a fall on an elevated roadbed. As I was knocking off the proverbial dust, something caught my eye. I had just missed another pile of acorn-laden bear scat. FT hikers were not the only ones using this path, an elevated walk-in-the-park route by contrast with the dense forests and cypress domes bordering the trail.

The Big Cypress portion of the FT ends at a gate dividing the preserve from the Big Cypress Seminole Indian Reservation. I went through the gate. Hiking the FT through Indian lands took preplanning. For starters, you need to be a member of the Florida Trail Association, then you need to sign a waiver indicating the planned dates of crossing the reservation. You send the waiver to the FTA, who forward it to the reservation, where it is kept on file. I surmised that this policy was in effect in case I should I fall and break a bone while on the reservation and feel moved to sue the Seminoles, who are now rich with gambling receipts. Damn trial lawyers, I thought. My father was a lawyer, though not a trial lawyer, and he paid for my upbringing; but the waiver wording inescapably triggered that thought anyway.

Just then, a turkey caught my eye. The jake with the bright red head was strolling in the sun. I was downwind and in the shade, therefore camouflaged. Another gobbler and yet another joined him from the trailside thickness. I stayed still but was eventually detected. Ahead, a pair of hawks called from an oak tree. A minute later the sun glinted on the white tail of a white-tailed deer as it bounded across the trail. The animals and birds I saw early that morning did not know they were not in a preserve but in a reservation, reserved for aboriginal Americans. They could not know how fast South Florida's human population explosion had closed in on them from both sides. The current state of the world was the only state they would ever know. They couldn't read in history books that a century ago Florida was the most rural state in the South, when this part of the Everglades was as far as the back of beyond could get, where Seminoles made their final retreat to escape the US Army. The animals I saw never knew the Big Cypress without the roar of vehicles on I-75 crossing the Everglades, or planes flying overhead, or the raised roadbed of a road-cum-Florida Trail carrying a lone hiker.

Something large was rustling in the brush to my left. A successful morning of wildlife sightings was about to reach its peak. A bear? My heartbeat upped a notch, then slowed as I realized the rustlings had a regular pattern. It was a man; a Seminole cutting palm fronds. He raised his blade—*whoosh*, then *whack*. He pulled off a frond, then gave it another whack, cleaning the limb end of it. The man carried a pile of fronds toward a truck; his buddy was doing the same. The Seminoles here once built chickees—thatched-roofed huts—under which to live, but now the chickees were used as picnic shelters behind people's houses or as showplaces for tourists. The raised track the FT traced, Jones Grade, widened into a full-fledged sand road and entered more civilized land, running between lemon and grapefruit groves. The neat rows of fruit groves contrasted with the natural contours of distant cypress domes.

The first house came into view. It was no primitive structure but a single-level ranch house, new and nice, with cars, trucks, and ATVs in the yard, testimony to the Seminoles doing well now that they have gotten into the casino business. Ahead were rows of winter vegetables being picked by non-Seminole labor, illegal or otherwise. The Seminoles were too busy running the farms and gaming businesses to be doing the picking.

The twelve-mile day ended at Big Cypress RV Campground, on Country Road 835. This was the beginning of a serious road walk but the end of the day for me. I wandered into the campground office to inquire whether they had room for a dirty Florida Trail thru-hiker. They did. I joined the only other tent campers in the place. The rest of the occupants were boxed up in RVs, the preferred mode for wintering retirees. On the way to my campsite a woman on a bike asked me if I was really going to hike the entire Florida Trail. With red hair and matching freshly pressed clothes, she had seen me at the entrance and overheard my explanation in the campground office. "Yes, I am," I said, and moved on, eager to clean up before getting too close to anyone.

A welcome shower, shave, and round of clothes washing took up much of the afternoon. Later, as I sat at the picnic table in the shade of a lonely palm tree, the woman on the bike came up, bringing a man with her. She had to show her husband the "dude who was hiking the Florida Trail." I then formally met Marlene and Ed, of Toledo, Ohio, down for a couple of months to escape a Great Lakes winter. Ed owned his own business and cleared the calendar for such timely getaways. They invited me over for a hamburger. We sat in the lee of their shiny gray RV, eating and talking until the mosquitoes ran us off. I returned to my campsite, happy to have made my first new friends of the trip but fearing that my backpack, left at the campsite, had become a training ground for an enterprising raccoon eager to separate me from the food I had carried from the Big Cypress.

The pack was okay. The swamp angels, however, were multiplying in the darkening dusk. I was battling skeeters with more clothes and bug dope when the night really began going downhill: my only tent-camping neighbors were dropped off in a big truck. Inside their tent they immediately turned on a TV with the volume so high that I don't know how they could stand it. Their two young kids began crying. The mother yelled for them to shut up, and the dad joined in on the act, cussing up a storm, which made the kids, now fighting with each other, cry harder. The man and woman then commenced yelling at each other so loudly and clearly that I could hear every word, and many were unsuitable for this book. When the yelling tailed off I was left wondering what life was like growing up with mean, ugly parents.

I crawled into the sleeping bag and rigged the mosquito netting over me. A TV program about movie stars blared in my ears, but no one else in the campground cared. They were all tucked away in soundproof, bugproof, rainproof RVs. Sleep finally came, then so did the rain. At first, it was the lightest of mists, and I just hunkered into the sleeping bag. The mist began sifting through the netting but I ignored it, and then it turned into a drizzle. Finally, I wearily retrieved the tarp from my pack and threw it over me, ignoring the pack's potential wetting. The conundrum now was that I couldn't lay the tarp over my head without feeling suffocated, as the wet tarp pushed the mosquito netting onto my face. If the netting lay directly on my skin, every little vampire could send its long proboscis through the netting and into me, as I found out after they had worked over my neck.

And so it went. I tried to sleep in the tangle of the tarp, bag, and netting. If I moved one way, water dripped down my back. Move another way and the netting would fall onto my face, allowing the mosquitoes to feast. Move another way and the wet bag would soak the clothes I was wearing. And my pillow, which consisted of the rest of my clothes, was getting wet, too. It took every bit of mental fortitude I could muster to sleep through this.

But all things must pass. Eventually the moon shone. The rain ended at 3:30 a.m. My bag, tarp, netting, and most of me were soaked. I went back to sleep, only to be awakened by a clanging alarm coming from the neighbors' tent. *Now* what? The alarm rang for five minutes straight before it stopped. Then it went off again, in snooze mode, until someone hit the button. And again. I had a few unprintable words of my own for them by then. Were they playing some kind of sick game? And then the TV came back on, just as loudly as before! I arose at 4:30, giving up on sleep. The cycle of crying kids and yelling resumed. A truck showed up at their campsite shortly thereafter, and off went the woman and the younger child. As she left, the guy in the tent said, "Remember what I told you." She replied, "Kiss my ass."

What a life. I felt sorry for them and sorrier for their children. I made coffee, packed my wet gear, and left Big Cypress Campground under cover of darkness to begin following CR 835. First had come surprises on the trail, and then surprises at camp. What surprises lay ahead?

4

Fields of Fire

Thus began my first road walk on the Florida Trail. A two-year construction project was blocking the L-3 Levee, which the FT normally followed, necessitating this road walk detour. I couldn't see much in the wan moonlight, walking up CR 835 against light oncoming traffic. My headlamp shone the way. My nose was getting all sorts of inputs, from the rich grasses at my feet to wafts of rotting decay from the ditch to my left. Cars increased by dawn. I retreated farther to the edge of the decently wide shoulder. My headlamp lit a fallen road sign indicating that I was now off the Seminole reservation.

Morning light revealed that the roadside was decorated with much more than grass. Litter was everywhere—beer cans, children's socks, hats, car parts, CDs, fast food wrappers, string beans, tomatoes, lighters, diapers, signs. Why would anyone would want to litter such a beautiful state as Florida? Alas, such roadside litter is by no means limited to the Sunshine State. While driving you may notice stray bits of trash in places, but walk along a road, and you will vow never to litter again. Yet this repulsiveness did underscore the beauty of walking—it forces you to slow down and inventory your surroundings, whether they include the feather coloration of a hawk or the exact composition of trash along CR 835.

I walked past a memorial to a teen killed in an auto wreck. It had been a while and the memorial was unkempt. Wind-strewn plastic flowers bordered a faded football jersey strung over a soiled cross. Candles rounded out the roadside tribute. Clouds kept the sun at bay as I made the seven miles along CR 835 and hung a right. The

Deerfence Canal ran alongside this road, and I joined the track atop its levee, pushing forward. A strong east wind whooshed in my ears and impeded forward progress. A fruit grove occupied the far side of the canal. More winter vegetables grew across the way. I reached the L-1 Canal, one of the operations of the South Florida Water Management District (SFWMD), which is charged "with managing and protecting water resources of the region by balancing and improving water quality, flood control, natural systems and water supply" from Central Florida to the Everglades. This amounts to a complicated job of trying to please a lot of diverse and sometimes opposing constituencies, while moving a lot of water around. Much of the Florida Trail in South Florida traverses SFWMD lands.

I took a break after twelve miles and proceeded to unload my pack at the G-342C water structure, where multiple canals met. Here I rejoined the actual FT track, which began a segment of following SFWMD-built levees beside canals all the way to Lake Okeechobee. I hung my wet items on a railing and took off my still-drying-from-the-Big-Cypress wet shoes. In the distance a large yellow vehicle came my way. It was a grader, leveling the track atop the levee bordering L-3 Canal. I waved as the driver approached. He stopped, turned off the loud machine, and opened the door. He said, "You hiking the Florida Trail?" He had obviously seen a few of my kind on this levee before. I told him I was. He asked, "Why?"

It was always the first question. I had whys. Here were a few: (1) To have an adventure with a certain goal and an uncertain outcome; (2) to connect the wild areas of Florida together; (3) to see if I could do it; (4) to spend the winter in Florida instead of the East Tennessee mountains; (5) to hike a long trail; (6) to write another true adventure story book; (7) to put a feather in my cap; (8) to promote Florida's master hiking path; (9) to get to camp out for months at a time. At any given time when asked why, I threw out a few of these.

Then I quizzed him, a muscular black man with a smile to melt the hardest of hearts. I knew he was not from around there. I'm an amateur "accentologist," and I was betting he was from the Peach State.

Sure enough, he had moved down from Georgia to Belle Glade "for the money" and had been there twenty-five years. I often ask non-native Floridians why they have come, and it mostly comes down to money or weather. He mentioned a water structure ahead that would make a good campsite. I proceeded to the site and found it commanding a fine view. Rotenberger Wildlife Management Area extended for untold miles. Rotenberger is the last natural expanse of the historic Everglades in this part of Florida. Willow marshes, grasses, and water-loving plants stretched for miles in every direction. Billowy anvil-shaped clouds built to the east and drifted slowly across the sky. A strong east wind pounded across the low-lying expanse. I continued drying my gear from the night before and caught up on trail notes.

A maintenance building provided shade. These water control structures did what their name implied. Usually located at the confluence of canals, they included gates that would allow water in or out, depending on the situation. It was not the wildest of campsites, but the view was well worth it. I lay on my back and watched buzzards fly high enough to suffer oxygen deprivation, while herons stalked prey in the canal. Other birds of all sizes played in the winds, flapping forward, then catching the breeze to shooting west with the blow. The winds brought showers, too. Lines of precipitation drifted across the expansive sky. I could see them coming for miles. All in all, it was a great place to spend a day of my life, on the Florida Trail.

At dusk, the wildlife nightshift came on. Frogs croaked in the canal. Mosquitoes searched for blood. Scattered lights twinkled to the north, miles distant. Greater Fort Lauderdale glowed to the east. Under the bug netting, in the bag, I began to itch. Somewhere along the way I had gotten into some chiggers. I found out later that Hans had been hit, too. The little red bugs ate me up good, leaving welts over my upper half. It was a price I paid for my insistence on sleeping out in the open. Sometime in the middle of the night a truck drove rapidly along the dike past my campsite. I'd been warned not to set up camp atop the narrow parts of the levee. There are better ways to go than being run over by a truck while camping on a levee.

I beat the dawn once more, breaking camp by headlamp. Swelling clouds formed mountains against the eastern sky as the sun pushed over the horizon, delivering a shaft of light between the clouds. Daylight again. For a frequent camper spending over 150 nights out per year, the nights can get long, especially in winter when the nights literally are long. I am always happy to see the sun again.

The twenty-hour respite from hiking had soothed the pain in my feet; but road walking with a heavy pack remained troublesome on those dogs, even though easier than watching out for underwater hazards. I kept north along the arrow-straight dike. The bird chatter picked up along the canal and overhead. Wading birds, songbirds, and flocks of fowl each put on their concerts. This part of Florida was decidedly less populated; few dwellings were visible from atop the dike. The footing was soft as it had recently been graded, revealing the identity of one nighttime visitor—a bobcat had left fresh prints in the dirt. I wondered if it had seen, heard, or smelled me and turned around? The commanding view was the best aspect of dike hiking. Rotenberger fell behind, giving way to pure agricultural land. Cattle pastures and winter vegetables spanned horizon to horizon. From this vantage point you would never know that to the east and to the west, on the coasts, were hordes of Floridians packed like sardines. The persons per square mile in these parts could be counted on one hand. Songbirds outnumbered anything else here. The sounds were ever present. The warbling, chirping, tweeting, and general singing would uplift even the most downtrodden hiker, or nonhiker.

I thought about how easy it was to start your day on the Florida Trail. Getting up in the morning, my outfit options were limited in number. No prancing in front of a mirror deciding on an ensemble. What I had for clothes was this: T-shirt, long-sleeved shirt with collar, fleece vest, rain jacket, one pair of short pants, one pair of long pants, two pairs of socks, hiking shoes, and flip-flops for camp. That was it.

My hair was low maintenance as well. Before the trip, my niece Jill had given me a shorter-than-military haircut. She called it a number two buzz, which referred to the razor number. This way, what little hair I had was not a nuisance, and the short buzz cut made me look less unkempt to strangers and during trips into town for supplies. I called it "wake up and walk" hair. The way it smelled after several days without washing—now that was another matter. Facial hair: I had shaved once already, back at the campground, and kept a razor in my pack for future cuttings. I had heard that lone males on the Florida Trail were sometimes treated as vagrants. Why should I expect different treatment? I was wearing the same clothes for days at a time and not bathing every day, a stranger walking through town with all his possessions on his back. That indeed smacked of vagrancy, though not too many vagabonds carry a solar charger powering a minicomputer enhanced with a portable keyboard, for writing autobiographical sketches about their wanderings.

The simplicities extended beyond appearance. I had one thing to do: walk the trail, wherever it led. My feet were eating up the miles, and I came upon sugar cane in all its glory, growing tall below the dike. Rising winds waved the stalks in unison, creating a background sound that serenaded one backpacker atop a linear monument to the power of the dredge. The whole thing was simply overwhelming. The complete alteration of landscape extended as far as the eye could see. Someone else might not see it, but the sheer vastness and completeness of the scope and reach of these Florida views rivaled a mountain scene—if you kept an open mind.

Dropping off the dike for a closer look, I was surprised at the cane's height and density. It didn't look as if you could turn all that luxuriant greenness into sugar, I thought, cognizant of my ignorance. Multiple stalks rose from impenetrable undergrowth. Cornlike leaves splayed outward from the stems. At its height, each stalk had tan-purple, ultrathin delicate flowers. I returned to the dike top. Smoke! Turning around, I caught the first glimpse of a sugar cane field burning. Whitish yellow smoke boiled forth from the once green fields. Expanding clouds curled and gathered and grew until they rivaled rain clouds in size. Cane fields are burned to eliminate dead leaves getting in the way of the harvest. Field burns are started on one side, allowing wild-

I returned to the dike top. Smoke! Turning around, I caught the first glimpse of a sugar cane field burning.

life to escape. The burns are short but spectacular, with a forty-acre field burning in less than a half hour. Modern mechanical harvesters are much more efficient than the old way of harvesting, whereby laborers used cane knives all the way into the early 1990s. Fields are harvested immediately after a burn. The average American consumes sixty-seven pounds of sugar per year. Personally, I am above the national average.

Cane smoke wafted overhead as I got some water from the dikeside canal, wondering what extra nutrients were in it. From the dike the panoramic views kept changing. The canal, the dike, and the road beside it formed a three-pronged northbound stripe that merged at the edge of vision, a place where I would be. From the linear perch, I didn't need a weatherman to know which way the wind was blowing. I could watch the clouds form, build, move, darken, and rain, mov-

Cane smoke wafted overhead as I got some water from the dikeside canal, wondering what was in it.

ing east to west. But once the clouds got this far inland, the rain had petered out to a few drops.

Cows and horses were grazing near the dike. With my passage they stopped and all stared in unison, moving their heads to follow my progress. Then they returned to their grass. I couldn't help but laugh, as I had seen this phenomenon while walking down the road with my backpack. Faces in cars stared out at me in much the same way as the farm animals gazed. Just before crossing County Road 835, I passed a shade tree mechanic practicing his art under a live oak tree. Two nearly identical cars—tiny Yugos, remember those?—sat in the yard. One was in parts and the other was getting fixed up. I looked for clues as to which was which but couldn't tell. Wrench in hand, the mechanic, too, glanced blankly up at me on the dike, then turned his head to graze on his engine.

By noon the heat was on, the air was still, the fields had lost their majesty, and the dike had become an elevated marching ground heading nowhere too slowly. It was time to take a break. A lonesome pair of palms bordered the bottom of the dike and I ducked under them, cooling down, revitalizing my innards with food and water. I had already gone eleven miles. I was wondering where to camp, but it was early. The grass around these palms was dead, stiff, and unappealing. Ahead was a water structure at a canal junction. The structure could provide shade. The place had merit: solitude, water, a level spot off the dike crest, but it was still too early. Against my own better judgment I went on, following the FT as it turned east, south, then east again, all along the L-1E Canal. I crossed CR 835 again. The canal, the road, and I were all heading to Clewiston, but the FT was taking the long way. The eastbound dike began to parallel CR 835—no camping here. The miles wore on and I wore down, walking in 85-degree heat in the open sun with teens of miles under my belt.

A hot wind gusted as I was approaching the end of CR 835. A post-hurricane illegal dump now marked where CR 835 turned north. A dead animal was reeking up the area, the effect exacerbated by the heat. The trail crossed to the south side of the canal. Just when I thought conditions couldn't get any less appealing, they did. Ahead, barren burned cane fields stretched for miles, with nary a tree in sight. I searched some scraggly brush near the trail but found no campworthy area in the cluster of devil's club, or cat's claw, or pullback. The nasty thorny bush has many aliases.

"Just keep moving and maybe something will turn up," I said aloud to myself. What else could I say? I blankly pushed ahead through cut weeds, feet scratching the ground, walking like a zombie, clad in a wide-brimmed hat and sunglasses. A lightly used paved road paralleled the canal on the south side, sporting an occasional eighteen-wheeler. The road decreased the "campability" of the area. I recalled the most repeated sentence in the journals of Lewis and Clark during the Corps of Discovery's epic journey to the Pacific Ocean and back: "We proceeded on."

Burned fields to my left revealed rich muck that was created by an untold period of growth and decay spawned from the annual overflow of Lake Okeechobee, the place where the miles-wide yet inches-deep Everglades sheet flow began. From the lake, water would spread wide and shallow, depositing sediment and nutrients during its journey to the Gulf. After Okeechobee was diked and this lower area canalized, the rich soil was ripe for farming, with no flood worries.

At last, grown cane fields once again bordered the path. I fantasized about climbing into the thicket, escaping from the sun, and hacking out a camp, but it would take too long with my Swiss Army knife. Long hot walks make bad campsites look good, or make unsuitable places look like campsites. I reached a junction of a railroad, a canal, and a car road. A side canal offered soft grass along its edge. The sun was now low enough for the grown cane to provide shade. This was the place. I dropped my pack, shed my shoes, walked over to the canal in my flip-flops, and walked into the water fully clad. Ah, sweet relief! And I was washing my clothes at the same time—talk about efficiency! I walked back to camp and quickly changed into other clothes before a car came.

Instead a train rumbled by. I called it the Sugar Cane Shortline Special. Emblazoned "USSC," which stands for United State Sugar Corporation, it carried cut and burned cane from a not-too-distant field to a processing plant in Clewiston. Deep into the night it chugged back and forth. The cane cutters in their specialized giant machines worked beyond dark, too, lighting the fields and the general area. I could complain about the noise of trucks and cars and tractors, but I was on their turf, and I was too whipped to care anyway. It sure felt good to be prone, watching occasional shooting stars and feeling the train rumbling the ground.

I relived the long day. Hiking is much more of a mental game than the casual observer may know. It seems simple and it is: put one foot in front of the other, keep going, and you will make the trail's end. The war is in your head—to stop or not to stop, to take a break or keep moving, to slow down or speed up, to quit or not to quit, to ignore the pain or succumb to it. And after you've had a tough day, to wake up in the morning and keep going. To believe you can do it, like the Little Engine That Could ("I think I can, I think I can"). Most limitations we have are self-imposed.

My dogs were still barking the next morning as I broke camp in the dark, to avoid any more stares of "Why is that bum camping by the tracks?" One more train rattled by while my little headlamp was lighting a coffee fire. The tracks were only forty feet away. I took a self-inventory: a scruffy man in his forties camping by a sugar cane field, heating water over dried sugar stalks fallen off the boxcars around creosote-laden discarded railroad ties, and steeping coffee that settled in the bottom of a blackened pot. I felt just like a hobo from the 1930s. "Might as well slink off like a hobo," I said to myself as I set out eastward, walking the canalside dike by the dawn's early light, pushing against a dew-moistened wind. Massive power lines formed a stringy silhouette against the breaking sky. The master canal of the Okeechobee system, the Miami Canal, sating the ever thirsty megalopolis, was soon before my eyes. The FT turned north here, toward Lakeport. I looked back and could see the train, heading back from the fields once again, passing the spot where I would never spend the night again.

5

America's Sweetest Town

Distant trees marked the village of Lakeport. Sunday morning was coming down but I was the only one to see it. A walk-through revealed a scraggly burg made worse by recent hurricanes. The word *scruffy* kept coming to mind. Ahead stood a land wall, a large dike. Was that it? The Big O, the dike that surrounded Lake Okeechobee? I couldn't believe it—already to Lake Okeechobee!

John Stretch Park stretched out before me on my side of the Big O dike. Run by Palm Beach County, this park was easily the nicest place in Lakeport. The town seemed never quite to have seen better days, but the park was immaculate. I decided to linger, enjoying clear, treated tap water. After the "Canal Zone" water, this tasted like a high-dollar elixir straight out of some protected spring. The shade of a picnic shelter was nice, too. The time came to "proceed on," and I clambered up the dike, easily four or five times as high as the previous dikes I'd seen—this might be the highest mountain I would climb on the Florida Trail hike, I laughingly thought.

The view from the top broke the moment. From there into the untold distance stretched Lake Okeechobee, the inland sea, the second largest freshwater lake wholly within the United States (Lake Michigan comes first). Seven hundred and thirty square miles. The water went farther than the eye could see.

Herbert Hoover Dike sloped to a canal bordering the lake. This canal is part of the Okeechobee Waterway, which, along with canals and rivers and some strategically placed dikes, allows boaters to travel from the Gulf side of the state to the Atlantic. Much of the inner portion of Lake Okeechobee is too shallow for deeper draft vessels.

The dike was thirty-five feet high, towering above Florida's Inland Sea. Between them, the Lake Okeechobee Scenic Trail—the LOST Trail—and the Florida Trail circle the lake atop the dike for 112 miles. This was the first "decision point" of the trip. Here I had to decide which side of the lake I was going to walk along, the east or the west. I chose the west side because it was more rural and quieter. Two more decision points lay ahead on the Florida Trail.

The scenic path attracted hikers and bikers. This part of the trail was especially alluring for bikers, as it was paved. Hikers with day packs didn't mind the pavement, but walking with a loaded back-pack on the pavement was a sure track to sore, blistered feet. The Army Corps of Engineers, which built the dike around the Big O, had planted a strip of sod parallel to the paved path, making it more foot friendly. But the grass was thick and lumpy and high, much slower going than the pavement. I therefore switched between the comfort-able grass and convenient pavement, pushed by a following wind.

The big three bad exotics grew in profusion on the landward side of the dike—melaleuca, Australian pine, and Brazilian pepper. Cane fields I had walked through stretched to the horizon beyond the exot-ics. The sugar cane processing plant on the south side of Clewiston had been visible rising above the fields for miles as I was walking through cane country and I could see it still. The Lake O dike walk would lead me right to Clewiston. U.S. Highway 27 roared beside the dike and seemed especially loud after the desolate sugar cane fields.

Four miles farther on, the Clewiston designated campsite came into view. Located on the lake side of the dike, the camp offered a picnic table and an open-sided tin-roofed shelter to block the sun. I dropped off the dike and unloaded my gear. At camp, the power-ing lake wind forced me to weigh down all light objects. Before me, boats sped up and down the lakeside canal for no apparent reason; but boating is only natural on a warm winter Sunday in South Flor-ida. The noise of the boats and US 27 irritated. The view, on the other hand, inspired. I sat back, eyes on the lake, watching the water reflect the clouds and the changing mood as day fell prey to night. Hurricane Wilma had nearly done in the shelter, covering it up with debris and knocking the roof on the ground. Luckily, my arrival was after the restoration.

That night the lights of Clewiston, but four miles distant, shone bright over the dike. The persistent east wind kept spitting showers, leaving me scrambling to keep my stuff dry. I decided to sleep atop the picnic table under the metal shelter roof, rather than in the sand that surrounded the camp. I leveled the table with some wood (it sloped toward the lake), lay down on my sleeping pads on the table—my lightweight closed-cell pad and Jeff's three-quarter-length backpacking air mattress—and then threw the sleeping bag over me. A steady wind kept me cool on the warm night, until it died down. Then the mosquitoes stormed in.

After hundreds of nights camping in Florida I should accept that swamp angels are possible or probable on any night, anywhere in the Sunshine State, but often I didn't take the trouble of putting up a defense and just hoped they wouldn't come. That night's poor logic centered around the wind keeping the bugs away. Three hours into sleep, I awoke in torment with a bit-up face. I leaned over to the pack, sprayed on some bug dope—the chemical kind that really works—and went back to sleep thinking about the second most used phrase in the journals of Lewis and Clark: "The mosquitoes were troublesome." Meriwether Lewis spiced up this phrase by spelling *mosquito* twenty-four different ways. Then they went after my arms, which were outside the bag. Wearily, I arose again and threw a string over the center beam of the shelter so as to attach my netting. It spread perfectly over the table. Presto, no more bugs.

To my surprise, a predawn start found me competing for space on the dike trail with four bicyclists! They were also trying to beat the heat on this warm morning. The sun lit the lake and the world around it, and a few sweaty miles later I was looking down on Clewiston, the seat of Hendry County. This was my first foray into a "trail town." Trail towns are spread along the Florida Trail's big brother, the Appalachian Trail. One such town, Erwin, is fifteen miles from my home in Johnson City. These towns were accustomed to seeing dirty, scruffy fellows carrying backpacks and heading into their stores and restaurants. Other trails towns, such as Damascus, Virginia, and Hot Springs, North Carolina, embrace hikers and welcome their economic effects. I doubted Clewiston thought of itself as a trail town. I was confident most residents had not even heard of the Florida Trail, despite it being in their backyard. Instead of being embraced I was half-expecting to be put in braces by the police.

I couldn't blame anyone for stopping the likes of me. Hence I had been courteously practicing my lines—"Yes sir, no sir, I'm hiking the Florida Trail, I am not a bum, here's my ID," and so forth. Into town I sauntered, down US 27, here called Sugarland Highway. I pulled up the sides of my hat, lending a safari-style look, imagining that this would make me appear more legitimate, like a "real" outdoorsman. Clewiston was a town from the 1960s. Small businesses just a step above ramshackle kept every item they had ever failed to sell, standing about in junk-strewn side lots or in the back. Chain stores were mostly absent, and homespun eateries were present. I liked that. The Dixie Diner offered 'gator and frog legs. Taquerías peddled Mexican specialties. Brenda's Place was a now-closed tavern.

Lining the sidewalk were a greasy old tire store and a few empty buildings with no discernible business whatsoever going on inside. Clewiston was a working man's town. Men worked with their hands, building and maintaining things. I saw no panty-waist office jockeys with pressed trousers, cell phones pasted to their ears, working in the idea and thought businesses. Uniformed men hurried into trucks and joined the others rumbling up and down the street. Everybody moved with purpose. Mine? To find a grocery store and make my first resupply.

U Save Grocery was across the street and a mile down the road. I stopped far from the front door to regroup. I changed from my disgustingly dirty T-shirt to my merely smoky long-sleeved shirt (despite the temperature having climbed above 75 degrees already). Then I deposited my valuables in my pockets and proceeded into the store, wondering whether wearing this long-sleeved shirt on an obviously hot day would be a giveaway that I was someone strange who needed to be watched. At the customer service desk I said, "Howdy. I'm hikin' the Florida Trail and I was wonderin' if I could put this pack somewhere and buy some groceries." The woman, in her sixties with white hair in a bun, looked neither shocked nor put out. She merely turned her head to the right and said, "You can put it right there." No big deal. I had worked up an unnecessarily unpleasant scenario in my head, all for nothing. Relieved, I went about getting grub. As I was checking out, the clerk and another employee came up to ask questions about the Florida Trail, where it went, and where I was from. They were truly interested. Perhaps the next FT hiker will have as pleasant a shopping experience as I did.

Leaving town with a much heavier backpack wasn't quite as pleasant. The burden was heavy on the shoulders and I sweated anew on the mile-long walk back to the dike and the FT. Along the way a city garbage truck passed by, with men hanging off the back. The moniker on the door was plain: "Clewiston, America's Sweetest Town." I didn't like to ask the men on that truck how sweet the sugar town of Clewiston smelled.

Since it was Monday, the trail and the lake were nearly deserted, except for the dead armies of the evil melaleuca tree that bordered the dike for miles. Extensive grassy wetlands stretched far into Lake Okeechobee. In the Big Cypress we had constantly had to look for an orange trail blaze every one hundred feet. Here you could go miles without seeing one, but the way was clear. I tromped along in the heat of the day, staying in the sod the whole way to protect my feet, and reached Liberty Point campsite.

The campsite was down from the lake, next to a canal on the landward side of the levee. This part of the state is laced with canals like a tracery of veins, interconnected in complex networks of channels ranging from arteries to capillaries, giving life to South Florida. The vein beside Liberty Point campsite was big enough for a dirty Florida Trail thru-hiker to take a bath or swim. The campsite, with a picnic table underneath a metal shelter, lay in a grassy flat with three palm

The Big O dike blocked the lake view at Liberty Point campsite but I could see south for miles.

trees for shade. The Big O dike blocked the lake view, but I could see south for miles. Across the canal lay the fields of fire. More yellowy smoke rose from distant cane burnings while closer fields stood green just across the canal. I could see the Sugar Cane Shortline Special chugging along, its black cars pulled by the solitary engine. It would honk at occasional road crossings. The Florida Trail had made three quarters of a circle, landing me just a few miles as the crow flies from where I had been forty-eight hours before.

The warm night preceded a foggy morning, and I continued around the lake. My only enemy now was that pavement along the levee. My feet were aching to get past Moore Haven, where the path turned to gravel. I had a choice: either walk the pavement and beat up my feet or get my shoes wet walking along the sloped sod. Wet shoes are no crisis for a backpacker and are expected, but my lightweight low-top shoes would wet through in short order if exposed to moisture, and wet shoes combined with dike hiking would surely result in blisters. So the real choice was between blisters and sore feet. I chose sore feet.

At Moore Haven, seat of Glades County, the trail detoured away from the dike and over a tall new bridge spanning the Caloosahatchee River. Walking toward the auto bridge I spied a low-running railroad bridge reaching across the river in one tenth the distance, with no detouring. I was briefly tempted to take the shortcut, but I was not hiking across Florida—I was hiking the Florida Trail, vowing to trace the orange blazes wherever they led me. I walked the new high span with its own protected walking lane and first-rate views that dwarfed the vistas from the levee. The Caloosahatchee, or rather the canal that had formerly been the Caloosahatchee, went arrow-straight toward the horizon. Moore Haven spread out below. The marsh of Okeechobee extended so far that no open water was visible.

Moore Haven was a little more dressed up and cleaner than Clewiston, at least in the parts of town where the Florida Trail traveled. The first business I saw was Miss Lillie's Laundromat, a low-slung white building with the door open. Patrons washed their clothes inside. I walked past, then halted, impulsively deciding to wash my dirty clothes. Rinsing them out in the canals wasn't measuring up, though it was better than nothing. I squeezed myself and the pack through the narrow door and adjusted to the light. Washers and dryers ran loud and hot while ten or more fans whirred to keep the room cool. The counter girl, a young black woman with smooth skin, looked up with little surprise. I instantly went into "the explanation," as I was calling it, despite her not asking for one. Then she sold me a small box of detergent and changed out some quarters.

We were having a few accent problems. After I said something in my Tennessee twang, she would ask, "Huh?" and I had to repeat myself. The same thing happened in reverse after she responded with her Caribbean tongue. I laughed at our communication foibles. Dropping my pack, I pulled out my grubby long pants and overshirt, threw them in the washer, then quickly tore off my shoes and surreptitiously tossed in my only socks (I had burned my other pair the first night), switching to my flip-flops. Some relatives joined the clerk. They all squeezed behind the tiny counter, talking, ironing, and sewing.

I moved that way to listen to the ear-pleasing singsong speech, a mix of eloquence and slang, then joined in the conversation. They were all from Jamaica, one having moved here as recently as two months before. The latest arrival said she had a green card and intended to stay in the United States permanently if she could; she was resentful of those sneaking in illegally and staying while she was doing it the legal way.

I washed and dried one set of clothes, then awkwardly asked if I could change in the bathroom so as to wash the clothes on my back. They casually obliged and I changed, though feeling that the whole experience was a touch bizarre. When was the last time you changed clothes in the bathroom of a laundromat? But when living out of a backpack, you gotta do what you gotta do; back in the Big Cypress Hans had called it a "life pack," since my whole life was in it. While the second load was washing I ran to a nearby store, happily going in packless and in clean clothes, to pick up some batteries.

Leaving Moore Haven, I felt the sheepishness of "urban backpacking" subside. I was getting used to the stares and was glad and proud to be hiking the Florida Trail, spreading a little news about this fantastic path that coursed through the state, including through Moore Haven. But would I be so happy about hiking the trail beyond this town by Florida's inland sea?

6

The Coldest Hour Is Just Before the Dawn

The sun blared back on the dike after leaving Moore Haven. Sol was both my enemy and my friend. I welcomed it every morning and cursed it every afternoon, then lamented its departure every night. It dried the dew off the trail, gave light and warmth, but then gave excessive warmth. It tried to burn my skin, penetrate my eyes, kick up dusty winds, fade my clothes, but it also made my wet clothes wearable and charged my minicomputer via the solar panel that rolled up into my pack when not in use.

Marshlands extended for miles from the dike, obscuring watery views, save for the canals on both sides of the levee. Sonorous and loud birdsong emanated from the sun-splashed marshes. I cleanly headed west, but sweat soon covered the fresh duds as heat waves shimmered across the burnished grass atop the levee. At least the trail was now a mix of gravel and grass and much more foot friendly. The bicyclists didn't like it as much.

Miles later, cane fields extended away from the lake and marshland continued ringing the inside of Okeechobee. I walked steadily, seeing no one, and reached the C5-A campsite, located at the junction of the main Okeechobee Canal and the L-41 canal. Couldn't they come up with better names for these campsites and canals? A few palm trees cast welcome shade.

I needed wood to cook the meat I had bought in town. A willow thicket bordered the camp and I went in for some fuel. After grabbing a handful, I reached for one last limb and began dragging it behind me. Dinner was destined to be good. Then my hand was on fire. I looked down and my left hand was a red moving mass. Ants! They were swarming over my paw, seemingly numbering in the thousands and biting in the millions. I threw the piece of wood down and hastily shook my hand until it was free of the little demons. My hand immediately swelled. Life's little surprises . . .

At dusk, the mosquitoes took over bug shift. After I turned on my headlamp, they were joined by some tiny nonbiting, light-loving bugs that swarmed onto and around my headlamp, landing on anything my light was focused on, like maps and reading materials. I ate the steak in the dark to keep the bugs from landing on the cooked cow and ending up in my mouth. This was a tricky affair since I needed one hand for swatting skeeters and two to cut the steak, one to hold it down with the fork and the other to work the knife in the dark. Oh, the delights of outdoor dining! Later that night, a front much-touted on the weather radio came in, blowing the skeeters away and cutting the clamminess from my sleeping bag.

Fifteen miles and eighteen hours later, I sat in the shade of the Indian Prairie campsite shelter, glad to be off my feet. This campsite, like the others, appeared little used. Courtesy of the front, a cutting north wind had blown strongly against me all day long, and that did matter to a backpacker on an open elevated dike. A three-mile early morning road walk between levee sections had not been too pleasant either. I passed many a snake that had come to warm up on the pavement, only to meet its demise from the things for which the pavement was designed. An element of the road walks was being subjected to the repeated stench and sight of road kill—'possums, raccoons, buzzards, deer. More power to those on road kill pickup duty. I did get to cross one of my favorite streams in Florida, Fisheating Creek. Now that's a good name for an even better waterway. It winds through cypress swamps, opens into small lakes, then closes back up to twist and turn through an area rich with wildlife, critters I hoped stayed along the creek instead of coming out to the road. The stream travels through the property of Lykes Brothers. Perhaps you have heard of them and their meat products.

Views of open water on Okeechobee had reopened at Lakeport, as the marsh had given way. On the landward side of the dike, Lakeport spread along State Road 78. Beyond that was cattle country. I approached Water Structure and Lock S-131. Here boaters could access Lake Okeechobee from the canal on the Lakeport side of the levee. The lock cut through the levee. Rick, aged fifty-something, was the keeper at the S-131 Lock. He was all smiles as I walked up out of the chilly morning. The first thing he said was, "Coming from Big Cypress?" Rick was obviously familiar with Florida Trail thru-hikers. Someone was docking through just after I arrived and he said, "Excuse me," and went inside to lower the water for the boater leaving the main lake. He came back out with a tooth-loaded grin, his mirrored sunglasses shining in the sun. We watched the water level dropping inside the lock, and once it reached the level of the canal, Rick again went into the tower and opened the other side of the lock. Away the boater went.

I asked where Rick was from, detecting an accent. He'd moved down from Hazard, Kentucky, and now he "worked two days a week and fished five." But the shifts were long, sixteen hours. "It's busy in the winter, but come summer, you just about fall asleep in there," he said, motioning to the control room. "Want some water?" I gave an enthusiastic yes, and he returned with a bottle that I chugged as he went on, talking about living in the nearby town of Okeechobee, where he had a mobile home. He testified that "a mobile home isn't the place to be during a hurricane. We had six hours of shaking like you wouldn't believe, 120-mile-per-hour winds coming from the north, then 120-mile-per-hour winds coming from the south."

I wasn't sure which storm he meant, but it really rattled his cage when "one egg-beater hurricane had churned up the lake, upsetting the fishing." Disturbances notwithstanding, he was still "living down here, just trying to catch the big one." I assume he meant fish, not hurricane. Rick obviously loved cutting up and having fun. When I asked whether he would move back north to escape the hurricanes, he said, "Noooo, too cold. If I move I couldn't come back here; property values have gone up 130 percent since the storms." I looked puzzled, thinking that storms would have driven people away. He went on, "All the people on the coast, they're moving inland to get away from stronger coastal hurricanes. By the way, your timing is good. They just mowed the levee. It was knee high last week." He told me about an eagle nest about a mile down, but I never saw it.

The wide levee ran northeast. The wind was blasting so hard that I had to lean forward into it, like a fullback plowing into a defensive line. The cold front had its advantages, such as clearing out the sky. Buzzards played in the updraft created by the wind blasting over the dike. Other buzzards lazed in the sun, apparently immune to Florida's increasingly hurried pace. A metallic-red speedboat sat in the canal below me, banked against a line of trees, out of the wind. Someone was fishing in the only place it was possible on this windy day, I thought. As I came closer, I was startled to see that the angler standing in the boat and tossing a lure around was a man of about sixty, fishing in a teeny bikini! Only in Florida. Judging by his rich skin color, I assume he was mainly working on his tan, of which I'd already seen see more than I cared to see. Most boaters waved at me, but this fellow ignored my presence on the dike.

A more appealing sight lay ahead, on the lake side of the dike: sandhill cranes. Florida Trail aficionado Betty Loomas had advised me to watch for wintering cranes beyond Lakeport. The talkative large gray birds with the red-blazed heads had once been a rare sight. Now they were all over Florida. The destination for the day was the Indian Prairie campsite, on the side of the levee away from the lake. A cattle pasture complete with cattle lay across the canal. Since the temperature was heading for the thirties, I set about gathering wood. Finding none nearby, I headed over the levee to the lake side and waded through deep grass leading to some dead and mostly fallen melaleuca trees. I gathered wood warily after the fire ant incident, and caution paid off. The first piece of wood swarmed with insects as I picked it up. Other, better wood was around.

It took multiple trips and high-stepping through waist-high grass to drag the fuel over the dike and back down to camp. The fifteen-mile day had taken its toll, and this last chore would assure a good night's rest. I absorbed the dying sun's rays then lit the fire and basked in its warmth, using it to cook dinner as well. The sun colored the sky pink, then red, before giving way to night. The north wind continued pounding across the pasture and canal. On a warm night, the combination of open campsite and wind would have been a great bug deterrent; instead it was a fairway for the cold blow, forcing me deep into my bag. The upper part I wrapped around my head with just my mouth exposed to breathe. What a difference a day makes. The night before I had tossed and turned in a hot and clammy bag, being nagged by mosquitoes. Now I filled my water bottle with boiling water, wrapped it in my jacket, and slid it to the bottom of the bag to warm my toes.

"They" say the darkest hour is just before the dawn. I say the coldest hour is just before the dawn. At 6:11 I arose and sprang into action, restarting the fire with small starter wood gathered for that purpose. I then tossed a fallen palm frond on the flames, which quickly torched, giving instant light and heat. Hot water became hot chocolate and hot coffee, transferring the heat of the fire to the water to me, warming me from the inside out. Then came breakfast. Oatmeal was on the lineup. It is an ideal backpacking food: compact, light, dried. It gives energy and is somewhat filling and comes in individual packets, which helps with portioning. It also comes in flavor variety packs and can be smashed for days at the bottom of a pack and still come out ready to eat.

But, to me, oatmeal is horrible. I call it "gagmeal." I have been eating it off and on over more than two decades of backpacking, but I still can't claim to like the stuff. I dropped two packets of cinnamon-flavored oatmeal into my pot of hot water and began stirring. The tan-colored flakes morphed into a reddish gruel that resembled—well, never mind. I shoved a spoonful into my mouth, and as usual my stomach quivered in protest. The answer is just to shovel and swallow as fast as possible to get it over with. One of the flavors in the variety pack purported to be strawberries and cream. It had little red food nodules that reconstituted into gummy blobs offering a rubbery textured alternative to the pasty cereal seed. I could hear my own commercial—"Try Johnny's oatmeal. It comes in assorted varieties, jaundice yellow, putrid pink, and bloating blue. It's gaggingly good!"

I looked forward to the day's hike—ten miles to Buckhead Ridge campsite. One reason for the anticipation was the condition of my feet. Overnight, every night, they were recovering from the previous day's punishment. The heavy pack and hardened dike would leave my dogs sore in the afternoon, but in the morning they were ready to go again. Having broken my left ankle and my right foot in two separate (nonhiking) accidents years earlier, I had turned potential weaknesses into strengths by literally walking those dogs back to health. I broke my foot in a jump from a ledge into a creek in the Smoky Mountains, hitting rocks instead of water. The first thing I did after getting the cast removed was go backpacking. It was only a four-mile hike on a relatively easy trail, but I was getting back on the horse, as it were. I broke the ankle playing pickup basketball.

This was the first day cool and windy enough to hike in long pants and long-sleeved shirt. The sandhill cranes didn't seem to mind the cool weather; they were squawking around on both sides of the dike. And dike hiking, even against a 10–15 mph wind, would still put me at camp inside four hours. The path led out to SR 78 to cross the Indian Prairie Canal by road bridge. Florida is blessed with so much water, and water plays a large part in the beauty of the Florida Trail. However, you have to traverse it to get anywhere. Up to a certain depth, walking through the water is an option, but deeper water becomes a problem. The Florida Trail Association simply did not have the assets, or in this case the authority, to build foot bridges wherever convenient. For that reason the trail often had to be routed over pre-existing road bridges. Leaving the bridge, I rejoined the high ground between the lake marsh to my right and cattle country to my left. My shadow, my only and ever-present companion on the grassy dikes, was cast long by rising sun. A gusty north wind pealed in my ears. The northeast-running track went straight to the horizon. When the dike curved, I could judge progress better, but here the straightaway seemed to go on forever.

Miles later, the first curve came near the town of Buckhead Ridge, which stood back from the lake. I crossed the lock that served the area. A crew of South Florida Water Management District workers was servicing the lock. I twisted my way past the crowd with but two miles between me and the Buckhead Ridge campsite. Soon the camp came into view, on the lake side of the levee. Palm trees bordered the tin-roofed shade structure. It lay in a wide grassy flat adjacent to the lake. Palms and willows bordered the shore, save for an open water stretch beside the camp. Ducks scooted around in the open water beside swaying cattails. Beyond that the lake stretched to the horizon—just another dramatic sweep on the Big O. The houses of Buckman Ridge were invisible on the other side of levee; the only structure visible from the campsite was the top of the town's water tower. No matter the length of the hike, it was always a relief to drop the pack for the day. The wind rose higher and stronger, whooshing and rushing and ebbing, only to blast anew. I battened down loose items on the pack.

I welcomed these cold and windy snaps. In a South Florida winter, periodic fronts punch down, bringing cold and blustery conditions that are followed by a gradual warming up. Despite the wind, the night would be warmer than the night before, with temperatures inevitably returning to their warmer norms. The fireside entertainment consisted of pulling cockleburs from my socks, the spiny little seed cases from weedy plants on the dike. As predicted, the weather was cool—in the forties. And no mosquitoes.

I broke camp in the dark, leaving Buckman Ridge campsite at first light. A chilly wind greeted me atop the dike. To my surprise, hundreds of bass boats were already assembled in the Kissimmee River below, lights shining in the dawn. A man on a loudspeaker was calling a number, then a name. A boat would zoom off, then another, another, and another. A fishing tournament was under way. I got a closer look while crossing the river, or at least the canal that passed for the Kissimmee, on the road bridge. A truck loaded with oranges rumbled by at the same time, flavoring the air but also shaking the bridges and nearly blowing me into the water. The anglers were heavily clad, each preparing to speed off into Lake Okeechobee, one more piece of evidence that the Big O really drew in the fishermen.

I was in no hurry, just walking along the Florida Trail. Where the lake met the Kissimmee River was a community of trailers, RVs, sheds, shacks, garages, and combinations thereof, forming winter shanties packed so closely that the occupants could have shared salt and pepper shakers at supper. These were the original Florida retirement communities, and some of the dwelling units looked sufficiently ramshackle to compete for the title of "The Very First Florida Retiree Home."

In places, the Kissimmee River was undergoing restoration to its original winding state, but this part was still perfectly straight, canalized and confined by levees. Authorized in 1992, the Kissimmee River Restoration Act will "restore over 40 square miles of river/floodplain ecosystem including 43 miles of meandering river channel and 27,000 acres of wetlands." But only 22 of the 56 miles of the Kissimmee Canal will be restored to a natural state. The rest will be maintained for flood control, which was the original mission of the Kissimmee canalization. Rumor held that its original purpose was actually to drain Disneyworld faster after thunderstorms. Was this pure urban legend? Reality or myth, I was heading for Orlando, perhaps to find out for myself.

7

What's in a Name?

The Florida Trail turned northwest here, following the levee built when the Kissimmee was first tamed. I was leaving Lake Okeechobee, the Big O, with a mixture of sadness and relief. I'd learned a lot in the past five days along the dike, but also knew that part of thru-hiking the Florida Trail was seeing places, then "proceeding on." Trailertown was also behind me, but one resident was still ahead. I could see the small figure in the slanting morning sun. As I got closer, the details came into focus. A skinny woman in her seventies, thick hair pulled under a baseball cap, was walking the dike with a little white yipping dog. The dog wore a sweater. The woman's head gave way to a pencil neck, which led down to a short pink bathrobe that hung way above a protruding nightgown bordered with a fraying hem. A knees-to-feet skin show was open to the elements. On her feet were blue slippers over white socks. I had never visualized fellow hikers looking quite like this. Reluctant to engage, I hung back as long as I could, then we crossed paths as she returned to Trailertown.

The cool morning made for great hiking and I was verily flying along the levee, which was not nearly as high or as sloped as the Big O's but still offered an excellent vantage for looking out over the cattle pastures, sod farms, and hay fields in the fertile valley of the Kissimmee River. I wondered how the ranchers and farmers felt about the restoration of the Kissimmee, the return of a river to a state known to their forebears, who once drove cattle. Ahead was the S65-E Lock, one more example of the SFWMD having no originality with names.

Boats moved along the river, literally going up or down it via the lock.

The last five miles before the lock were the last miles of levee walking for a while. The trail aimed north away from the lock and went to State Road 70. The Florida Trail normally continued forward on a quiet county road, leading to another lock where the trail crossed to the west side of the Kissimmee. Unfortunately, that lock was being worked on, blocking the FT dike. This forced a rerouting, which forced a road walk. I turned left, heading west on SR 70, headlong into the traffic. At least I had a nice large median to work with. Cars and trucks hummed and blew by. Trash presented the same disappointing scene I'd found on other roads. The only upside was getting a leisurely look at the orange groves beside the road. These fruits looked ready to me, and I thirstily lusted after them. I entered Highlands County by crossing the Kissimmee on the Billy Bowlegs Memorial Bridge, built in 1966, according to the metal plaque; these are the things you learn by walking and not driving the roads. A short while later I turned into the Kissimmee River Fishing Resort, with twelve miles under my shoes. This was the only place to camp on the road walk, or else face a twenty-seven-mile day from backcountry campsite to backcountry campsite. Twenty-seven miles didn't sound like fun.

From the road I eyed the place, fronted by a decrepit convenience store, the kind you weren't sure was open. Behind it, among stately live oaks, were scads of RVs, sheds, and small trailer homes, as much a retirement community as a campground. Most of the trailers had not moved in years. Sheds had grown up around them. A line of mailboxes confirmed permanent residency for many folk here. I walked into the store, where a friendly woman stood behind the counter. My two abiding impressions were of all the tasty edibles around and of dyed black hair. I asked if she had a tent site for a Florida Trail thru-hiker. She got on the phone and in walked Bobby, a friendly and fast-talking ex-Mississippian. He stuck out his hand like a salesman and began rapid-firing questions at me. I followed the bespectacled ball cap wearer, whose mind worked faster than his ears. He shot out question after question before I finished answering. Affable Bobby led me to a live oak with a lush grassy floor. Trailers were all around and the road was in view. I was the only tent camper. But it was here or nowhere.

Bobby did his best to make me feel at home. I thanked him for his time and headed for the showers, to make the most of the one amenity campgrounds offered that was truly enjoyable. Later, clean, I whiled away the cool windy afternoon, feeling like a backpacking exhibit. I ambled over to the convenience store to wait for Hans and Jeff, who were coming to meet me following our phone conversation. (My cell phone was powered by the solar charger.) Jeff had ordered another air mattress for me on the Internet and was to deliver it. This ultralight job weighed a mere nine ounces, replacing Jeff's heavier mattress that I had borrowed to stand in for the one I had lost in the Big Cypress. Behind the store was an assembly of residents engaged in a sort of a daily impromptu bull session. I walked up with an ice-breaker—"Is this a meeting of the Kissimmee River Liars Club?"

Everybody chuckled, and a retiree sitting in a beat-up golf cart spoke up: "Only when we're talking about fishing." I joined the Liars Club. One blonde mom was waiting for her kid to be dropped off by the school bus. Another guy, toothless, drove a work truck with a magnetic sign on the side; he slurred as if he had been working on his buzz instead of buzzing down trees in his horticulture endeavor. They grilled me about hiking the Florida Trail. As always, people wanted to know why. Why would one want to walk across the street, let alone walk the length of the state? This time my response was "to see Florida up close and in slow motion."

Hans and Jeff showed up at dusk, straight from work. I appreciated their delivery. They soon had to blast back to the greater Fort Lauderdale area. I hoped to see them later on the trail, but only time would tell. That night I moseyed over to the Rancher, a homespun restaurant next to the campground. I lost control at the all-you-can-eat catfish special and crawled back to my campsite so full that I groaned in my bag that night, despite the new sleeping pad. Limitless plates are the stuff of backpackers' dreams.

Fast-talkin' Bobby had said he'd be making coffee at the store at 5:00 a.m. I stumbled from my camp toward the store. A light was already on. Perhaps coffee was brewing. To my surprise, eight or nine men, all retired, were crammed into the tiny depot, delivering accents that spanned the thousand miles from Michigan to New York as they were sipping java and conducting the morning session of the Kissimmee River Liars Club. They welcomed me, and we were soon all bantering together. They were very encouraging and enthusiastic about the hike. I appreciated that. We said our goodbyes and I proceeded on, leaving the Kissimmee River Fishing Resort in my imaginary rear view mirror.

Light was coming, and I hadn't gone a hundred yards before a van hurriedly pulled over. A woman wearing baggy clothes and looking hasty hopped out and ran across the road, asking, "Are you a Florida Trail thru-hiker?" I said yes, and she offered a ride to eliminate the road detour. I wanted to accept but was determined to hike every foot of the FT, even the road walk detours. She shook her head and said, "Suit yourself," and she sped off, smoke belching from the box on wheels. Residents familiar with the FT knew a thru-hiker when they saw one. Settling for the road walk, I passed cattle ranches and sod farms, wondering how they got the sod from ground to truck. The route turned north at Highlands County Road 721, a very quiet road.

What can you say about a long road walk? I was certainly getting to see some of Florida's cattle country up close and in slow motion. Cattle rank high, with citrus and timber, in filling the state's agricultural coffers.

An audience of red-winged blackbirds lined the pasture fences, singing me onward. The Florida Trail was blazed, even on these road walks, plus I had trail maps and the companion guide. I had bought a complete series of maps from the Florida Trail Association, more than forty maps, depicting the trail from end to end. These were invaluable, not only showing the way but detailing mileages between points, with thumbnail trail sketches and important information about supply points and campsites. I had also bought the *Florida*

Trail Companion Guide for Long Distance Hikers by Sandra Friend. This book, which had some weight, gave more detailed information than the maps, but like any book, it was running a little behind on up-to-the-minute information, such as trail rerouting, store closures, and prices. Still, the information was more than worth its weight. Between the maps and the book, I had a rough idea of where I was going, where to camp, and where to resupply. But hiking the actual hike should, could and would trump decisions based on books and maps.

Nearly nine miles later, the sun was high and the afternoon clouds were building. I was relieved to reach some bona fide trail hiking in the Basinger Water Management Area, along the Kissimmee River. The FT passed an old homesite just inside the management area. Here, tangerine and grapefruit trees were drooping with fruit. I helped myself. The tangerines were freshly flavorful. After gobbling six in a row, I began to wonder just how many would be too many of a good thing. A backpacker's diet is a strange thing. But this was a real treat, trailside fresh fruit that I didn't have to carry. The FT wound among stately live oaks, many hurricane damaged. More woodsy meanderings led to a clearing and an abandoned orange grove before the trail returned to forest and the Basinger campsite, located in an oak hammock a hundred yards from the Kissimmee River.

The fourteen-mile day had left me thirsty so I headed for the river, which came into view after I had crossed an open field. Then a little problem cropped up. Between me and the open water was a fifty-foot-wide mat of thick waterweeds. How was I going to get through that? Another surprise took me at the edge of the land. Someone had laid some concrete block leading toward the river. Steps, perhaps? Would they hold? I put one foot down and the block gave way, sinking into the mat and muck. In the interests of getting only one shoe wet, I backtracked to terra firma and took off my foot coverings, then returned to the mat. I began walking barefoot on the spongy vegetation, each leg sinking halfway to my knee before the stringy vegetation would briefly hold me—if I kept moving. To stop was to sink. It was like walking on top of canned spinach. I did the walking mat

An oak fire burned hot as I boiled water for coffee.

dance for fifteen feet, decided this was a losing proposition, cut my losses, and returned to land.

Now, how to get water? I couldn't just push my water bottle into the mat, for the stirred-up water had a lot of "land" in it. My tongue was a dustbowl. I decided to push the mat down with my foot and let water collect as it rushed in to fill the void in the mat, then wait for the heavier particles to descend. It worked! But the result was still messy, with debris and floaties throughout the aqua. I returned to camp and strained the water through a coffee filter before slaking my thirst. Just as bad campsites look better at the end of a long hike, bad water looks good after extreme thirst.

An oak fire burned hot as I boiled river water for coffee. Outside the nighttime firelight, in the brush, a constant rustling was in progress. Armadillos. These creatures were seldom found north of the Rio Grande before 1850, but they have since expanded their US range to include most of the Southeast and nearly all of Florida, save for the southern Everglades. Florida's armadillo explosion started separately, with an accidental release from a small zoo in 1924, followed by a second breakout from a circus in 1936. In a sense the animal is just following the lead of the opossum, which also migrated this way from South America despite conditions that seemed hostile. Armadillos are fast breeders. Only limited rainfall and a constantly cold winter with January temperatures averaging 28 degrees or lower will stop them. If you live anywhere from New York west to Nebraska, south to Texas, or at any point to the Southeast, don't be surprised to find these plated diggers chew up the ground near you.

In the morning I left the Basinger tract and crossed another parcel of SFWMD lands. This was the EEEE parcel, where the trail undulated over old row-cropped lands before entering a gorgeous grove of live oaks. The respite was short-lived. Soon I was back on the road, after wrangling through a barbed wire fence, tossing my pack over the barbs then slithering between the wires.

The FT entered the Hickory Hammock Wildlife Management Area just beyond the Istokpoga Canal. Now a foot trail for days, it wound into oak hammocks, between pine trees, through grassy clearings, and beside open wetlands. I absorbed the scenery, and my pack seemed to have lost five pounds. The live oaks formed green cathedrals held by brown support beams. Acorns covered the ground in the thousands.

The path joined the Old Basinger-Sebring Road, built in 1949. The elevated track was long abandoned and is now the preserve of hikers. Massive oaks stretched out their arms horizontally, forcing me to duck beneath them in places. Judging by the footbridges over waterless streambeds, I took it to be a dry year. The forest became denser, a place where palms, oaks, and saw palmetto thrived in profusion. The Florida Trail was but a narrow thread winding amid their lushness, and it kept moving from such thickets to more open areas, forming a changing mosaic of environments. My hat kept going on and off with the changes in sun and shade. A deer quietly grazed in one clearing. My footfalls alerted the beast, and it darted into the impenetrability, a safe place where no man could follow.

The afternoon had warmed after my lunch stop at Hickory Hammock campsite. I was sweating more than a sinner on the way to meet

The respite was short lived and soon I was back on the road.

Satan. The ground at my feet was dug up in places, the rootings revealing that wild boars called this area home. As wildlife managers in several states have found, this non-native pest is difficult to eradicate. For me, the pigs made following the trail more difficult where they had torn up the trail bed. An ongoing forest burn complicated matters too, but this was still much easier than tracing the orange blazes back in the Big Cypress. Blackened in hopscotch patterns, low vegetation was still smoldering in spots. Most of Florida's natural forests are fire dependent. They need occasional low-level burns to keep their natural character.

I contemplated the import of hiking the Florida Trail. What made it special was getting in on the front end. Thousands had hiked or tried to hike the 2,100-mile Appalachian Trail. More than two thousand people make an attempt each year. Many had thru-hiked the Continental Divide Trail and the Pacific Crest Trail, both ultralong paths, but fewer than one hundred people had thru-hiked the Sunshine State's master path. That was also why I was not seeing other thru-hikers, though this was the season for doing it.

The FT moved closer to the Kissimmee, which at this point was no longer canalized, but back to what it used to be like. I walked the edge of the river prairie. It stretched to a distant line of barely discernible trees across a watercourse that looked more like vegetation than water. I wondered if you could walk on that. Palm islands rose from the marsh. Distant flocks of wading birds fed in the shallows, then all exploded into the sky at once for reasons unknown to me. Flocks of other birds flew in unison, up and around then beyond my view. The trail continued along the edge of the prairie as it skirted a private fenced ranch to the west. Then it once again threw some challenging terrain my way. Here grass grew in huge irregular clumps, up to my knees in places, forcing me to be mindful of every footfall. The river shallows sometimes extended across the trail, forcing wet crossings on floating grassy mats and slushy stretches that were neither land nor water. But it wouldn't be Florida without a little wet hiking under a sultry sun.

Boardwalks and bridges helped ahead. A twenty-five-foot-high bridge offered a panorama of the Kissimmee, including the main river channel below, where the flow was surprisingly swift. The prairie looked watery from this bird's eye vantage. A long boardwalk beyond the bridge must have cost a pretty penny to build, so I expected clear sailing to the Bluff Hammock trailhead, just ahead. I pushed on to another surprise: thickets of Caesar weed blocking the trail. This head-high brushy weed is thornless but has little seeds that catch on everything, including hair, shirts, and especially socks. An exotic, the plant likes disturbed areas. Boars disturbed the soil, and the invasive weed came in after them—one more reason to eliminate wild hogs. I had to fight my way to the trailhead and spend several minutes pulling off the Caesar weed seed. No sense in spreading it farther.

The path was in much better shape north of the trailhead, and soon I was pulling into Mosquito Hammock campsite. You'd think anyone would be apprehensive about camping in a place with such a name, but after seventeen miles I was ready to stop anywhere. The camp was nestled in live oaks with an understory of too much Caesar weed and a few fruit trees. And it had a pitcher pump well that

A twenty-five-foot-high bridge offered a panorama of the Kissimmee; the flow was surprisingly swift.

delivered some of the best water I'd drunk yet. No sulphur taste, no swamp taste, and no floaties. I sat at the campsite picnic table, watching tiny fruit flies work over fallen and rotting grapefruit. The sky had clouded and rain was a possibility, so I hung up my poncho/tarp, rigged the mosquito netting, and hoped for the best. That night the owls hooted and coyotes howled over the peepers, small frogs that make a pleasant nighttime hum.

As it turned out, the rain did not arrive until after I had left the next morning. A long boardwalk allowed dry passage just beyond Mosquito Hammock. More boardwalks spanned the beds of intermittent streams flowing down to the Kissimmee from the gentle plain above, where cattle grazed. The skies darkened further as I made my way north along the Kissimmee, entering Avon Air Force Base. A hiker permit station marked the entrance; even as a Florida Trail Association member, I had to fill out a permit. You couldn't be too careful in this post-9/11 world. The air hung still, warm and heavy. Crows called from the trees above, breaking the morning silence, rejoicing in their unbridled freedom. I surprised a 'possum, still lurking about past dawn. Unlike the hogs, this species does no harm. It is our only marsupial and sports the 70-million-year pedigree of having coexisted with dinosaurs. But the 'possum is less than lovely; I invited it to get back to South America.

The woodlands on the base, combined with those of the Kissimmee Prairie State Preserve across the river, effectively create a huge wildland. The Florida Trail drifted through rich oak hammocks scattered with palms, occasionally leading into open riverside prairie or into a saw palmetto–gallberry plain. Sunshine State city dwellers may not realize there are such people-less expanses in Florida. Avon Park Air Force Range started out as Fort Kissimmee during the Second Seminole War. Zachary Taylor, the future president, set up Fort Kissimmee in 1837 while heading down to Lake Okeechobee to battle the Seminoles. Later the area was settled by cattle ranchers until World War II, when they were relocated to make way for the Air Force Range we have today. Many homesites and a nearby cemetery remain.

A rabbit darted in front of me just before I arrived at the main Fort Kissimmee camping area. The dark skies had let out just a little rain, but I was not concerned now, as the camp had a picnic shelter for refuge. I dropped my pack after the ten-mile day, calling it quits before noon. The skies soon lightened and I took advantage of the solar shower available here, which provided only lukewarm water, as sunlight had been in short supply that morning. Normally, the sun's energy is collected by solar panels and transferred to batteries, from which it is drawn to heat water in a suspended tank above the shower area. I washed my hiking clothes and muddy socks and set them out to dry.

A couple came up in a camouflage truck. They were on-base volunteers, helping keep the camping areas clean. Jack and Joan hailed from Pennsylvania. A toned figure looking ready to go back to boot camp, Jack enjoyed being on the periphery of the military scene, since that had been his career. They offered some crackers and coffee as I showed them my camping gear and explained life on the Florida Trail. I was becoming more prideful of the experience and the trail itself. And I was understanding one of the meanings of the hike: the trail connects the disparate parts of the Sunshine State together, and walking the trail is a way to make sense of Florida's far-flung divisions.

Avon's military jets started flying later that afternoon, in advance of some heavy clouds. The noise and power they demonstrated during their exercises was amazing. They would fire off a round, noise echoing off the clouds before landing without an explosion. Dummy bombs, I guessed. The jets returned that night, and I watched their lights swoop and whirl. Hikers were smartly advised not to touch any munitions they found.

Breaking camp early certainly had its advantages. The air was cool, and the sunrises were amazing. Overnight, another welcome cold front had moved through. I was on the move by sunrise, my warm hiking engine cooled by the north wind. Cardinals darted in the thickets. Deer bounded in a wet meadow. Pines began to mix in with the live oaks, adding another component to the vegetational variety. Just a foot or two of elevation could mean the difference between hiking in live oaks, pines, or prairies. This area was clearly the most scenic since the Big Cypress.

The first rays of the sun lit the Fort Kissimmee Cemetery. Massive live oaks, draped in Spanish moss and topped with resurrection ferns, hung over the burial ground, where descendants of those who once lived here were still being interred.

Later I entered Orange Hammock. It was easy to see how this place got its name. Orange trees aplenty were scattered in the woods, offering more citrus than a Florida Trail thru-hiker could consume on the entire hike. But I tried, having felt no ill effects from the earlier tangerine overdose. I had mastered simultaneously hiking and peeling fruit, but it left my hands constantly sticky. Wild fruit trees provided easy snacks. Tangerines were my favorite. I never ate a grapefruit, assuming wild ones must be even more sour than cultivated ones. Generally the fruits of the wild oranges and tangerines were less sweet than the cultivated varieties.

The scenery changed like a set in a fast-moving play. A live oak cathedral opened into one of the longest prairie clearings yet. Then just a few steps later, the FT rose into a pine-palmetto forest. A fence marked the north end of Avon Park Air Force Range. I climbed over the stile, entering Kicco (pronounced "Kisso") Wildlife Management Area. Here the trail turned away from the Kissimmee River and began to work around Tick Island Slough; its moniker suggests an island covered with ticks and surrounded by stagnant water. Is that any more appealing than Mosquito Hammock? I continued to walk in solitude. The last backpackers I'd seen had been in the Big Cypress. Some bicyclists were on the Big O dikes, but since then the trail had offered the utmost solitude, unless you count the road walks.

Cypress trees grew tall and noble at Tick Island Slough, unlike the twisted and fragile-looking hiker bridge that spanned its waters. It has since been replaced. I chanced the span, making it across Gum Branch with little reverberation, and stopped for a water break. The water was covered in a layer of scum, with no discernible movement. I knocked back the scum, dipped the water bottle in, and drank. The water tasted fine, with little hint of the sulphury flavor or taste of decay prominent in some Sunshine State waters. That was the funny thing about aqua here—I could never predict what it would taste like based on how it looked.

A flock of turkeys skittered from my path onto the prairie's edge. Wildlife moves about more in the early morn. Oak-pine woodland thrived on the higher ground beyond Tick Island Slough. The cold front had painted a vivid blue backdrop against which the green pines contrasted. Sunlight filtered through the oaks, delivering rays that dappled the forest floor. I startled another flock of turkeys, which took off through the trees with furious flapping. A small group of about five deer kept just ahead of me, their white tails bounding away into thicker woods each time I got too close. The Kicco Wildlife Management Area seemed to be managing the critters with success.

The trail went around the slough and resumed a northerly course, with the greater Kissimmee River to my right. Still higher ground marked the old Kicco townsite, on this bank of the Kissimmee. Cattle now populated the ghost town. The modern amenities under the live oaks were picnic tables and grills placed there by Florida Department of Environmental Protection, which manages the area. Kicco came into being with the Kissimmee Island Cattle Company. The town, with post office, saloons, a school and more, existed only from 1916 to 1926 as a staging point for cowboys before driving their cattle to the Gulf Coast at Punta Rassa (now Punta Gorda). From the port, the bovines would be shipped to market. Kicco went the way of the cattle drover. I walked the narrow concrete paths, which were about all that remained. This was one town that did not roll up the sidewalks when everyone left.

A tight gathering of buzzards beyond Kicco told me death was ahead. Half wanting and half not wanting to see what the victim was, I looked anyway. A dead boar lay on its side in a watery ditch, matted wet coat torn open. A lone buzzard was perched atop the carcass, pecking away at the flank, and other buzzard brethren were nearby. The scene was pretty disgusting, and the odor of the dead boar just about knocked me out. Nature isn't all sweet flowers and singing birds. Buzzards must have a warped sense of smell.

My ears worked next—a snort! Then I saw them: five differently colored wild boars shot across the trail. I had finally seen some live boars after miles and miles of seeing their tracks and rootings. This crowd looked as if they were leaving the funeral of their buzzard-topped brother. Rattlesnake Hammock lay ahead. Another foreboding name. An area of lush live oaks grew amid the scrub lands around it. It was easy to see why the Godwin family had chosen to homestead this parcel. They ran a cattle operation here for several generations.

I took a shady break at Rattlesnake Hammock, and as I moved on, the FT opened to a barren-looking plain beside a relic dike that had not been removed during the Kissimmee River restoration. It was as if I had been instantly transported to West Texas. Only a few piles of cow manure and fewer cows broke the monotony of brown grass. The north wind blew hard across the plain, likely made of spoil from digging the canal. I walked over to the irregular dike and looked down on the Kissimmee. The river was smaller here, heading south between bordering waterweeds.

The desolate country continued for a while, but the trail eventually moved west into low marshy areas, remnants of the old Kissimmee. Ahead I came to an oak hammock, and the trail wound on to Long Hammock and my camping destination. Unfortunately, the creek just before Long Hammock, which was to deliver campsite water, was dead dry. My pack held no water; as a weight-saving measure, I avoided carrying any. This meant going to Plan B (one has to be able to roll with the punches in the outdoors), even though I had logged seventeen miles already. About a mile ahead, according to the Florida Trail Association map, was a ditch with water.

I wandered on, traversing an area that had been burned. The palmetto understory, about waist high, had already greened up, but the trees were still leafless and black, an interesting if uncampable sight. Ice Cream Slough looked as if it had been canalized and was not appealing, nor was the terrain around it. But the aforementioned ditch was indeed flowing. I walked along it, searching for a camping spot that offered shade for the afternoon but something to block the cold north wind for the night. A wall of saw palmetto near a live oak worked perfectly.

By dusk I was in full regalia: T-shirt, long-sleeved button-up shirt, fleece vest, and jacket, sitting with my back to the trunk of the oak, its limbs stretching above me. The horizon line was still light enough to form a backdrop revealing the outlines of nearby palms. That evening lying close to the fire, I studied the *Florida Trail Companion Guide*, conjuring up images of what the path ahead would be like. Of course, what you imagine and what you eventually see don't always match.

8

How to Turn an Easy Day into a Hard One

February came in cold. Scattered frost whitened the ground as I departed in the murky half-light. Fog gathered in low-lying spots. The Kicco trailhead was a half mile distant. I made my way through a tight passage in the wooden fence. This passage was narrow and V-shaped to prevent bicycles, ATVs, horses, cattle, tricycles, and perhaps aliens, camels, or banana slugs from getting through. It may not have served well to keep out stray cats, but it came close to restraining some hikers. I rose up and squeezed and bulled and bored through, then got walking. Passing a ranger's house, I traced a dirt road out of the WMA and through an entity known as River Ranch, a resort-type place where visitors could imitate Old Florida cracker cowboys for big bucks.

The early morning sun beamed bright, warming the chilly morn as I arrived at State Road 60, four miles distant from camp. My light pack, devoid of food, made walking easier. The Florida Trail headed east on SR 60, but I had to turn west for a planned resupply. The Kissimmee Corner Country Store was 0.4 of a mile distant, according to the *Companion Guide*. I could see the building.

Trucks were rolling by as I was thinking about food and what other necessities to purchase. From a little closer, the store looked as if it might yet not be open. No cars were visible. I might have to wait a little. Closer yet, and it looked as though a red plastic fence encircled it. Uh-oh. The windows were boarded. Closed! I walked faster, hoping reality would intervene in the mirage with a busy store reappearing, but it was not to be. I crossed the road to the store and dropped my pack in disbelief. What to do now? I stood helplessly, pondering the next move, telling myself to relax and come up with a solution. The pack, leaning against the plastic fence, caught my eye. Something was awry. My sleeping bag was gone—just when I thought things couldn't get any worse.

I needed food, but I really had to find the sleeping bag and my fleece vest, crammed in the sleeping bag's stuff sack. I threw on the pack and rapidly backtracked toward Kicco, hunting for the fallen bag. Obviously I hadn't heard it fall. My pace sped up as the worries grew. I backtracked the four miles faster than on the outbound leg. Standing at the road near the Kicco ranger's house as I neared the trailhead was a thick-set fellow of around sixty, whom I guessed to be the ranger.

"Have you seen a black sleeping bag?" I vainly asked, still rushing for the trailhead, figuring the bag must have been dislodged from my pack as I squeezed through the fence. "Nope." he said. I hurriedly explained I was hiking the FT, and he tailed me to the trailhead. Sure enough, on the ground lay the bag.

Whew! One problem down. I relaxed at a picnic table while Warren and I began to visit. He talked very slowly. He wasn't the ranger but the father of the ranger's girlfriend and was over from Hillsborough County. Warren offered to drive me to the River Ranch Country Store, a carefully cowboy-styled convenience store. I thankfully accepted. "Limited supplies with higher than average prices," the judgment of the *Companion Guide*, was an understatement. I didn't even bother to add while shopping. Enough grub to fill half a saddlebag added up to fifty-eight dollars! On the way out, I said to Warren, "I didn't know you could spend fifty-eight bucks at a convenience store without buying beer or gas!"

We headed back to the ranger's house, where I met Warren's red-haired wife Glenda and the wildlife officer, no-haired Jeff. Jeff had recently become a ranger after a business career in South Florida. He had quit his job and was wondering what to do when he saw a job posting for a wildlife officer, and he said it was the best move he'd ever made. We sat around a fire drinking coffee as the fit and fully uniformed Jeff got ready to leave on assignment. Glenda made lunch, which I greatly appreciated, then Jeff took me down to SR 60, where I had been hours earlier, eliminating a second backtracking. I'd already logged eight miles, but netted only four FT miles, as I headed east on SR 60 over the Kissimmee River bridge under dazzling sun. I contemplated the morning's events. If the store had been open I would never have met Warren, Glenda, and Jeff, a fine group of people. Life's little surprises.

A paving project did not enhance the road walk, but the men doing the paving bantered back and forth with me over the machines, the cars, and the fresh smoking asphalt. I told them I was walking from Miami to Pensacola via Jacksonville, another way to explain the route and extent of the Florida Trail.

Car noise died as the trail turned north along a sun-splashed dirt road leading into Three Lakes Wildlife Management Area. The sun punished me and my thirst was rising. I had consumed the Diet Coke from the rip-off store. In the hubbub I had forgotten to replenish my water bottle and was now paying the price. The trail slithered north through a low-slung palmetto prairie, which offered no barrier to the sun. Looking for something positive, I briefly—ever so briefly—appreciated the scenery, then moved to appreciating the quality sunglasses and hat that were musts on the FT. I'd broken the fifteen-mile mark but had to push forward. Without water or shade, stopping was purposeless. The prairies seemed to go on forever.

I looked on the FT map, then on the reverse side of it. The reverse side gave written thumbnail sketches of trailside landmarks. For this area, at a particular mile mark, it said: "Cross ditch. Usually dependable water." Now what, let me ask you, is *usually* dependable water? The stuff is either dependable or not. "Usually dependable" means not dependable, and so it proved. The ditch was dry. This would have been a great time to go into a funk, perhaps to lie down on the trail and beat my feet and arms on the ground like a toddler—*Waaaah! I want water!* I was concerned, as Three Lakes WMA had a reputation for having little water during dry times, and this was a dry time. I pushed on through the knee-high sun-cooked vegetation, finally en-

The Florida Trail slithered through a low slung palmetto prairie, which offered no barrier to the sun.

tering a lush hammock of live oak and palm. The shade was dreamily welcome. I stopped for a minute in the gorgeous sunless jungle. Songbirds were twittering overhead with melodious throats. They knew where the water was.

The path mercifully stayed within a line of trees, providing some shade. My tongue was as dry as a well without a pump. Ahead lay a muddy muck depression. Maybe? The surface was covered with green duck moss. I walked over and contemplated how to get water; mud was suggestive, but it was still just mud. The afternoon was getting late. Fodderstack Slough was five miles away and I faced the possibility of going that far to camp. I did the only thing I could do: "proceed on," Lewis and Clark style. Then, just ahead, a clear stream silently crossed the trail! I immediately veered left and found a campsite in nearby palms, dropping the reloaded and once again weighty pack. Two and a half quarts of water later, my thirst sated, I began to make camp. And that water was fine, too, completely funk free.

The sun dropped west as I leaned happily and exhaustedly against a palm. Overhead, flocks of small songbirds whizzed by as one, just above the tree line, heading to roost. They made a surprising amount of noise simply by collectively flapping their wings; not quite loud enough to wake the dead, but loud enough to command the attention of a whipped FT thru-hiker. The first flock was startling, then the numbers of flocks startled more. Flock after flock after flock. What a show! Just before dusk, an owl landed in a tree about thirty feet from camp, its outline unmistakable. I stilled and watched. The bird would swivel its head and then just perch motionless. Finally I had to move, to get a little wood for the fire. The owl did not fly off. Instead it came a little closer. Dark filled the sky and I never did see the bird leave, but owls hooted to each other through the evening, probably remarking upon a thirst-riddled hiker crossing the plains and prairies of south-central Florida.

The weather rollercoaster was heading back up on the new morn. Warm, windy, and partly cloudy. The FT headed north, then west, traversing a mosaic of ecosystems, including junglelike oak and palm

The sun dropped west as I leaned happily and exhaustedly against a palm.

hammocks bordered by wide prairies, gold grass waving in the early morning breeze. Stands of trees became distant mountain ranges across the open flats. Palmetto prairies were lonely places, seemingly fit for neither man nor beast, with an aura of utter desolation and complete absence of humanity, the land of fire and water. They need fire to maintain themselves, but they flooded in rainy times. Lightning strikes in spring and summer historically started fires that kept these prairies open.

Three Lakes WMA is also noted for its wildflowers, and true to form, it offered more colorful blooms than any other place since the Big Cypress. The path crossed a forest road bridge over flowing Fodderstack Slough. After this, it continued merging in and out of ecotones, never long in any one situation, whether as live oaks, pines, palms, or grassy clearings. The FT picked up an elevated tram route that bisected a seasonally wet area and came within sight of Lake Jackson. The open waters called, but I pushed on to Parker Slough. The slough offered deep moving water near the road bridge that spanned it. I stopped and took advantage, stripping off my clothes and washing off the grit and grime, then rinsing out my hiking clothes.

Parker Slough was a bit cool, but refreshing. I hung my clothes to dry, then dried off uneasily in the sun myself, hoping no one would come by while I was in a state of nature. Real men don't take towels out backpacking. Do you suppose a wildlife officer would buy that line? I could see it now: ticketed for being as naked as the beasts that roamed these woods. No one came by. Soon I donned my long clothes, while waiting for the other duds to dry. I nixed camping here due to auto accessibility of the campsite. I call it the Nine O'Clock Syndrome: get settled in at camp, and at 9:00 p.m. up will come some beer-drinking hell raisers, leaving you few options. If you have no escape vehicle of your own, it's better to camp where no cars can reach.

I had a lot of recourse at this point. I chose to press on as the afternoon grew cloudy and very windy, despite trepidations about water. The companion guide promised water in a creek four miles ahead.

Was it usually dependable, I wondered? The forest was burning not far beyond Parker Slough. The blackened forest floor bordered the trail as smoke wafted around. I trucked on, not too worried that the low-level blaze would impede progress. On the contrary, some of the walking was wet as the FT passed through a cypress dome. Other domes lurked in the distance, but soon I was crossing Canoe Creek Road.

This road marked the second Florida Trail decision point. At this junction, the FT split into western and eastern corridors. The western corridor was a work in progress and had many road walks connecting wild wooded areas. The eastern corridor worked around the eastern suburbs of Orlando but was mostly in backcountry areas and also traversed the entirety of the Ocala National Forest, one of my favorite areas in the state. This decision was easy. Head east. The creek was just ahead. I worked through some pines and saw a line of cypress trees delineating Canoe Creek. Cypress trees need water, at least part of the time. The watercourse was dry, just a bed of damp soil. Luckily, a small dark pond was within sight of the trail—ideal for a camp.

I found an elevated flat between the creek and pond in the forest of spindly pine, with a nice tree to lean against. You need a tree to lean against, otherwise you will be lying down. The eerie smoky and cloudy afternoon turned to hazy dark evening, after a brilliant sunset. The wind continued to pound through the night, and I smelled smoke off and on.

Light was not yet in evidence as I stumbled along the dry creek bed in the morning, feeling my way down the path. The weather radio had predicted an extended rain event. The clouds were already here, that was for sure. The hot murky dawn never had a chance to brighten as sinister clouds kept lowering until they seemingly skimmed the tops of the pines or dipped to knee-high palmetto prairies. Mosquitoes nagged me. This was the first time the swamp angels had bothered me as I hiked, landing on the back of my arms and biting. I finally had to stop and spray my arms and back with bug dope. The path wound between cypress domes as it aimed for the Florida Turnpike. I could hear the rumbling road as I worked through saw palmetto. At the turnpike, eighteen wheelers and passenger cars whizzed by, but soon I was walking under the tollway, tracing a forest road.

Three Lakes WMA extended along both sides of the interstate as the Florida Trail kept a northeasterly track, now winding among scrub oaks and turkey oaks. The low light spread forlorn over the area; not even a bird was chirping. At least I did not have to worry about sunglasses, hat, or sunscreen. In my homeland forests of southern Appalachia I rarely used these, but only a fool would go without them here. There wasn't here, and here wasn't there, and I appreciated each place for what it was.

A blast of cool wind brought me back to the here and now. The breeze was refreshingly cool, though it portended trouble. To the north loomed a black horizon, coming ever closer. It was fixing to rain. I threw my feet a little farther forward with each step to make US 441. After that first blast, the air remained hot, dead, and still. I pushed north on the road as a light drizzle ensued. If I continued north, US 441 would take me over the Smoky Mountains, right through Newfound Gap near my Tennessee home. But I was going up it only two miles before turning east onto Florida Forever property, a private eco ranch that allowed the FT to pass through its lands.

The drizzle evolved into a downpour. I watched it sheet across a palmetto plain. I donned my poncho/tarp for the first time and it worked pretty well, even inside out, as I had erroneously put it on. (It always pays to test and use gear at home. I hear some people actually do that.) The inside-out factor made the snaps on the sides harder to work. Ahead, the Forever Florida campsite was visible in pines to the left. I aimed for the camp, reaching the shelter, a three-sided affair with an open front, complemented with nearby restrooms, a spigot, a fire pit, and picnic tables. I unleashed the tarp and spread out my gear in the wooden refuge, watching the water fall. The weather radio announced a tornado watch for the area. Before me, lightning flashed and rain pounded. A particularly nasty cell framed with an electric blue aura drifted across the southern horizon. I was very glad to be in the shelter, having endured but an hour of real rain while hiking.

To the north loomed a black horizon coming ever closer. It was fixing to rain.

The storms came and went through the afternoon and into the night, and I watched the whole show from underneath the shelter, looking out the open side, which faced west. Talk about good timing—this was the first trail shelter I'd seen the whole trip! I can't help it if I'm lucky.

I awoke at 5:00 a.m. and all was still. Not even any dripping from the trees. I took the chance to make a quick cooking fire with wood I had gathered between storms the previous afternoon. Coffee, hot chocolate, and gagmeal were quickly consumed, and I packed up, ready to depart at dawn. The weather radio, however, announced a line of storms entering Osceola County, where I was, and sure enough, another round of rain commenced. After watching the rain for a long spell and seeing no end to this term of imprisonment, I finally unfurled my bag in boredom and napped for a while.

At last, near noon, the rain quit again. Two inches of precipitation in nearby Melbourne, the radio said. I resumed the FT, now flooded in many locales. Streams were high and ponding was common both on and off the trail. Not surprisingly, I saw no other human that day. A two-inch rain keeps people inside. Beyond Forever Florida property, the Florida Trail headed into Bull Creek Wildlife Management Area.

The rain-washed landscape fearlessly displayed its colors. Funny how things change. A day ago I had been looking for water, but today I would be walking through it for miles. As I slogged, the water was seeping into the soil all around me, recharging the aquifer below. The area needed some rain. The orange FT blazes stood out boldly against the reddish brown trunks of the pines. Bull Creek was a wet and lonesome place. A constant wind penetrated my ears all the dark day. My shoes sloshed loudly through the water. Bull Creek was managed by St. Johns Water Management District. I had changed watersheds at some point, crossing some imperceptible high spot. Before, I had been traversing lands that drained south and west, through the Everglades and into the Gulf of Mexico. Now I was in lands that drained into the St. Johns River and north to the Atlantic Ocean near Jacksonville. A watershed moment.

Nursery Slough flowed freely among its palms and oaks and wax myrtles and ferns, its tea-colored waters bordered by white sands. Feet and legs already wet, I just walked through it. A few miles later I was at Little Scrub campsite. This camp was set in a sand pine forest open to the sky overhead. Skeletal sand pine trunks, relics of a burn, rose above waist-high vegetation, which blocked an increasingly cool north wind. The weather rollercoaster was heading back down tonight. I gathered wood, made a fire, and dried my socks using the hot water bottle trick: boil water over a fire, pour it into your water bottle, then stretch your socks over the water bottle and let the heat push the moisture out of the socks. It usually takes a couple of rounds of reheating the water for each sock, but it gets the job done with no chance for burning. I bedded down behind some thick brush for shelter from the wind.

The next afternoon the batteries in my camera died. I put in some new ones bought at River Ranch, but they were dead too, though I had probably paid double for those. The grub box was getting low

Skeletal sand pine trunks, relics of a burn, rose above waist-high vegetation.

again anyway; resupply was indicated. That night I sat by the fire, thinking about this book. How do you explain the solitude found in the back of beyond, amid a scenic landscape, where you can hear the crackling of the fire, broken only by the sounds of two birds passing overhead, each flap of each bird's wings clearly audible. Such are the rewards you can reap on the Florida Trail.

But it's no fun putting on wet shoes on a 40-degree morning. I'm not sure where that fits into the Florida Trail Rewards Program. It would have been useless to dry the shoes during the night, as the rains were sure to have flooded the trail ahead; I had dried the socks to keep my toes warm in the bag. It would be several days before this water ran off. When you are going on a long-distance hike, you must extend your *discomfort* tolerance range. Putting on wet shoes on a 40-degree morning was the price of solitude. This was the first morning when I looked forward to getting hit by the sun to warm me up.

I followed the FT north along the edge of Bull Creek. Sandy portions of the trail had been hardened by the rain. It was Sunday morning and the hunters were out. I heard a few pops in the distance and decided to put my red, white, and blue Confederate flag bandana around my hat, just for insurance. The hunters loved being out here as much as I did. They just enjoyed it in a different way.

The FT joined an old logging tramway from the early 1900s, lending this section a historic air. Shallow wet canals and pure wetlands bordered the elevated track. The tram had been built with occasional low spots, formerly bridged, to allow the waters dammed by the tram to flow into Bull Creek. Narrow-gauge logging railroads once hauled the cypress and other woods from the area. Now, palms, pines, and some oaks grew on the narrow berm, forcing hikers around and between them. I sloshed into the water where the bridges had stood. The trail went off and on the old tramway. I met a father-son hunting team, out for squirrels. I whistled lightly to get their attention. The big-gutted father, from Melbourne, said the place looked very different after the storms of late. They hadn't seen a squirrel. Neither had I.

The man was right—the downed vegetation *was* excessive. Fallen palm fronds, limbs, leaves, and other detritus that had once floated in the rising water of heavy hurricane downpours had bunched up and settled in heaps as the water receded. Much debris was on the FT itself, where hikers were gradually crushing it down. Ultimately it would decompose, recycling its nutrient content. Hurricanes and their effects are a normal shaper of Florida's ecosystems. The state's large human population centers have to deal with this premise, for there will be hurricanes as long as there is Florida. Ahead, the tramway path bisected a cypress swamp. The brooding beauty of the area was alluring, but I had to keep an eye downward, as many cypress knees protruded from the tram road. While watching the ground intently, I also noticed the old crossties in the soil. The ties ran perpendicular to the direction of the tramway. In places, roots of trees grew in the same direction, forced to grow that way by the crossties themselves.

Beyond the bridging of Yoke Branch, the FT split. One way was the high-water route; I stuck with the regular trail since I couldn't get any wetter unless I fell in. The track joined another tram road. The old ties were visible here, too. The woods were dense and offered a closed-in atmosphere—remote, yet utterly unlike the remoteness of the open expanses of the sawgrass or palmetto prairies. The FT now left the trams for good, and my cold feet appreciated the dry footing. However, the dry ground was short-lived, as the path headed back into a swamp, then through more pines before reaching Crabgrass Creek watershed. The day's last mile was pure knee-deep slogging, mostly a result of the rain.

Crabgrass Creek flowed clear and reddish. The sun refracted in the water, revealing the underwater universe at my feet. Small maple seeds, designed to flutter through the air to reach a suitable sprouting spot, landed on the creek surface, swirling and turning in the flow. Maples often thrive in these lush wet swamps of the Sunshine State. Was my intended campsite going to be flooded? The trail reached a series of bridges spanning what I took to be the primary channel of Crabgrass Creek. The narrow bridges were wide enough only for foot travelers to cross, but old ties and pilings upon which one footbridge was built revealed long use of the crossing by more than hikers.

Jane Green campsite was on the first high ground beyond the creek, not flooded, set in an open pine stand. The sunlight was welcome on this cool windy day. Still going down, the weather rollercoaster and would reach a low point after dark. This was Super Bowl Sunday, the day when Americans consume the second most calories, after Thanksgiving. My fare would be noodles and some hot chocolate. The bag of trail mix I ate for lunch was my last snack food. Breakfast had been gagmeal, of course. Even prisoners were having better Super Bowl parties than I was. But I was where I would rather be, out on the trail, warming by a piney fire. I listened to most of the game before hunkering down in the sleeping bag, less than full to the gills. But the menu was fixing to get better.

9

Hot Fries, a Mural, and a Manuscript

The chilly morn made for fast travel. Two miles later I walked into the gleaming morning sun, east on US Highway 192, which was being turned into a divided highway. The construction area made for open safe walking and the road crew didn't seem to mind. This was the beginning of a thirty-mile road walk. The Florida Trail Association formerly had an agreement with Deseret Ranch to route the trail through their property atop a dike, but it had ended, and the long road walk began. After breakfast I was foodless until a small fruit stand ahead, where I could get a little bite to last for the walk. The stand was at the intersection of US 192 and County Road 417. Hand-painted wooden boards touted their fare—hot boiled peanuts, oranges, etc. I read each sign with hungry anticipation. More boards were ahead, nailed onto the store's windows—the place was closed.

You'd think I would have learned the first time. It would be a long hungry walk. I turned north up CR 417, which bisected Deseret Ranch. At the point where the Florida Trail turned north, it was as close as it would get to the Atlantic Coast. CR 417 was quiet, save for the pasture-preferring songbirds. A car passed only every little while. Even the cattle were few and far between. I walked hard, making the most of the cool morn. This was Mormon country. A few roadside houses even had cars with Utah plates on them.

Cool morning became hot afternoon as the FT followed Nova Road. At Taylor Creek, some bank fishermen were just unloading their cane poles, bobbers in hand. The fat black men were going for catfish, they told me. The afternoon was wearing and I called my friend Aaron Marable. The twenty-five-year-old skinny white artist was in Orlando, where I would spend my first night off the trail. He would jump in his truck and be here in a while. I walked a little farther, doing my usual wave as the infrequent cars went past. One contained a Florida Fish and Wildlife officer, who immediately turned around and came back to have a word. Dennis Harrah asked where I was going. I gave the usual responses, also mentioning that I had reeled off twenty-two miles already that day. The burly fellow smiled, reached over, and dug into a cooler, whipping out a canned soft drink. While I guzzled, the big smiler told me about his dream of hiking the entire Appalachian Trail. He would attempt his goal soon, after getting in his thirty years with the state by Halloween. I offered to bring him a soft drink when he passed near my house on the AT. It may happen, as we exchanged cards.

Quiet Nova Road gave way to State Road 520, which was also being widened. Orange traffic cones bordered dirt swaths outside the old two-lane track. Trucks and other heavy machinery churned. This obstacle course was not an ideal place to get picked up, I thought; I pressed as hard as possible, despite my sore dogs, to get beyond the mess.

Then came Aaron. He was smiling while whizzing his truck between the cones. Having knocked out twenty-four of the thirty road miles, I was admittedly relieved to be done with the day's road walk. Give the FTA time, and the trail will be back in the woods. We traveled speedily on toll roads to downtown Orlando. At least it felt that way to me—I'd had been averaging two to three miles per hour. I could have done without the traffic and hustle and bustle, but my attitude changed when we arrived at his girlfriend's condo. Tara's fine quarters reflected her Italian heritage, as did her dark mane. The orderly discussion of her day revealed how on the ball she was. Tara had changed from her nursing scrubs into a fresh set of nursing scrubs. She obviously appreciated their comfort. I did the cleanup routine, including a clothes washing, then Aaron and I went to the local grocery store for resupply. The after-work food-buying rush was on, and the tension was palpable in the checkout line. Everyone was ruining the now in hopes of saving a little future, hoping it might be more relaxing. When you are walking, fifteen seconds don't matter.

The three of us enjoyed a fine dinner, talking around the table, eating on matching plates. I'd been eating with a spoon that didn't quite go with my smoke-blackened pot. Tara was improving her nursing status and had just gotten a new job. Aaron discussed the latest mural he was painting. His living consisted of going into people's houses and painting scenes on walls. It took a lot of guts, I thought, to do such grand projects as these, making sure the eye of the homeowner and the eye of the artist saw the same thing. But Aaron was good at what he did. He delivered.

Sleeping in a bed that night was easy after the long day, the longest yet on the hike. My string of twenty-three consecutive nights of backpacking was broken, but the break was worth it for the enjoyable evening. The morning traffic crawled into downtown Orlando, contrasting with our speedy outbound progress. We shot back to CR 520, and Aaron dropped me off at the construction site. As I began proceeding on, I noticed a woman operating a rolling machine, leveling the asphalt, as she had been doing the day before. Her eyes popped when she saw the same guy with a backpack, the guy she had watched being picked up in front of her the day before, now being dropped off the next morning, same pack, same clothes, in the same spot.

The last six miles of the road walk passed like Elmer's Glue. Part of the pleasure of walking a new route is seeing new scenery evolving ahead, but I had already traversed this road twice by car in the last few hours and knew the landmarks leading to the Beeline Expressway. Tosohatchee State Preserve, the next natural area the FT explored, was just ahead. I happily sloshed down the narrow trail, still wet in places from the rain, through what I called the golden forest. Tawny wax myrtle leaves, tan palm fronds, and blackened palm and pine trunks bespoke recently burned woodland. Fallen bronze pine needles added yet more burnish to the mix. Green touches of growth were already emerging. Overhead, the slender sylvan needles of unburned tall pines glittered against the blue sky.

WATER UNSAFE
FOR DRINKING

The pump well
at Tiger Branch
campsite

Tiger Branch campsite relaxed me after the ten-mile day. I thought about how rushed everyone seemed in Orlando. Was that the way to live? Is this the point to which we have evolved? People just don't take their time any more. They let their time take them.

I headed over to the Tiger Branch campsite pump well. A sign announced: "Water unsafe for drinking," with a few other disclaimers in fine print. Why have a pump well if the water is unsafe? The signs were there to stop people from lawyering up and suing because they got sick from the well's offerings. The state forest was doing hikers a favor by providing the pump well, yet they had to assume a defensive posture.

I was still a little beat up after the long road walk and sat motionless under the swaying pines and palms, regenerating for the hiking days ahead. Yellow pine pollen was dusting all that sat still for very long, including me. Spring was under way. Yet another front rolled in that night. The rainless air mass sent a reinforcing shot of cool air, keeping the weather rollercoaster down. A series of fronts was expected to continue sweeping into Central Florida. Because of the strong wind I doused the fire that night before retiring and found a flat spot amid some myrtle bushes, to block the blow. The sky cleared overnight, revealing a waxing moon, dropping the temperatures into the thirties by the dewy morning.

I rekindled the fire, boiling water for coffee, and dried the dew-moistened sleeping bag. The golden forest ended at a sandy forest road; these often act as firebreaks in controlled (and uncontrolled) burns. Here the Florida Trail picked up an elevated tram road winding amid tall pines. Wildflowers peeked their colors above the ground clutter, especially pale and purple violets. The tram ran deeper into woodland, imperceptibly losing elevation enough to enter a richer, thicker forest of palms and oaks. My hiking heat was just enough to counteract the chill. I was boosted by the sunny rising day and untrod trail, revealing the natural beauty of the Sunshine State on a day that had never been lived before. Who knew what awaited? I expected good things. The Tosohatchee Preserve was sure to deliver on its beauty. It felt great to be alive and in Florida.

A negative outlook might render things this way: "The dark morning chilled me as I searched for foot space along the overgrown narrow trail, sometimes bordered by chest-high brush, awash in dew, which wet me as if it were rain and scratched me like a cornered cat. It was only a matter of time before I met some standing water, sure to soak my feet. I would then be forced to walk in wet shoes and socks for the rest of the day." But I wasn't feeling that way. Yes, the wind blew cold, my feet got wet, and the dew drenched my arms, and the overgrown brush occasionally scraped my bare arms and legs, but I was alive: feeling, seeing, hearing, smelling all that the Tosohatchee Preserve had to offer. I could have been battling for a parking space to enter a building full of irritated co-workers, endlessly beeping phones, and a boss to order me around. Pick your poison. I'll take wet feet and a few saws from the saw palmetto.

The morning ramble led to the northern boundary of the Tosohatchee and reached the town of Christmas. It was named for Fort Christmas, a short-lived fortification near here, established on Christmas Day, 1837. The fort has long since deteriorated, but a replica stands near the original fort site. Christmas, less than a mile square, was an assemblage of ramshackle and not-so-ramshackle trailers and other portable buildings, and a few constructed houses, most with overloaded orange trees that whetted my appetite. I worked west through the sun-splashed grid-laid streets, making my way to a convenience store disguised as a grocery store under the rather grand name of Christmas Groceries. Minding the place were two older women, born in another country I could not determine, though I guessed at Eastern Europe. I walked in and smiled, still with the backpack on, and announced, "I'm hikin' the Florida Trail, mind if I get somethin'?" Of course, the woman said.

I explored the fare, determined to beat the convenience store prices. Surely they had an item or two that wasn't exorbitant? I ended up with nothing but a newspaper and a Diet Coke until I saw a display stand of chips, two bags for three dollars. They were big bags, too. Aha! The display had been well picked over, however. The only kind remaining was Hot Fries. I decided on one bag and strolled to the counter to make my smart purchase. "It's *two* bags for three dollars. You must get two bags to get the bargain," the counter woman said. I walked over and got the second bag. "How long you been walking?" she asked in her thick accent. No other customers were around, so we conversed a while, and I realized from her body language that the other woman in the background did not understand English. The phone rang, and the one who couldn't understand English began talking in a language that I in turn could not understand. America, I thought, the land of opportunity, where you can come over and buy a convenience store. Bring your relatives.

Two big bags of Hot Fries in hand, I walked on through Christmas, passing a store with a signboard outside stating that it was 321 days until Christmas Day. I opened the first big bag and munched the overprocessed foodlike substance while walking. Talk about making you thirsty. I chugged Diet Coke, laughing at the image of the roadside chip-eating, Coke-drinking, presumably health-conscious hiker. I was headed for Seminole Ranch, another state-owned wild area. At the preserve boundary the Florida Trail entered deep woods along a sand-bordered meandering stream, where tea-colored water curved more than your average swimsuit model. No ditch this, it was a genuine creek, cutting the deepest channel I had seen yet. The forest remained lush along the stream and along other "tea creeks" that the Florida Trail bridged as they flowed to meet the St. Johns River.

Moss-covered palms rose vertically, while the spreading live oaks provided horizontal structure. The resurrection ferns were alive and well atop the live oak limbs, the rain having revived them. Overhead a woodpecker casually knocked on an unseen trunk. Ground ferns grew in masses, fluttering above the slightly spongy earth, which was swathed in oak leaves where the ferns lost sway. The miles passed rapidly to a quiet forest road. I turned off to an unnamed, undesignated campsite set in a tall shaded copse of live oaks towering over denser vegetation. Hiking brings on thirst as surely as spring brings flowers, so I got water out of a ditch by the campsite. I referred to the ditch as a "linear wetland"; it made the aqua taste a little better.

That afternoon I hung out in a sunny clearing near the campsite to stay warm. Time is funny at campsites. Sometimes it passes slowly, sometimes fast. That day it was fast. I think it depends on how tired you are. When whipped, I tackled camp chores as rapidly as an osprey swooping for a fish. When excess energy was available, I might lie around for hours before wood-gathering time. At dusk hundreds of ibis flew west to roost for the night. They flew just above the trees with loud wing beats, their avian velocity making their own bird-speed sonic booms.

As night came on I reluctantly began delving into the second bag of Hot Fries, even though the corners of my mouth were red and raw from chomping down the first bag. I decided the Hot Fries would be my dinner. I sat in front of the warming oak limbs, burning in their steady fashion, and methodically forced the "linear chips" into my mouth. They were bad to begin with, just food vessels carrying salt that burned my tender mouth corners, and they didn't get any better. Spontaneously I tossed the mostly uneaten bag into the fire, to prevent me from eating the balance. The plastic wrapping melted onto the fries, then slowly burned to a crisp. Who was the winner here? I really showed the convenience store industry, getting a food bargain, buying too much of what I didn't want, then toting it for miles, only to toss it into the fire, uneaten. I brushed my teeth, but the taste of Hot Fries remained.

The fire was the best yet of the hike. Fallen oak limbs provided ideal wood. Oak burns slowly and heats extraordinarily well. I kept scooting closer to the fire until I slipped into the bag for the night, Hot Fries still lingering on my palate.

I entered Orlando Wetlands Park the next morning. The city of Orlando has made the most of its wastewater treatment area, managing it very successfully for wildlife, and it is now a destination for bird lovers and more. I saw deer and pigs, too. The FT nearly encircled the park and worked its way along the floodplain of the St. Johns River, a lush forest with a spongy floor. This was as close to the St. Johns as the FT would get. The wet trail and thick woods made for slow going, especially when I knew the path paralleled a dirt road barely beyond view. But the purpose of the Florida Trail is to take in the scenic places, not just to get from point A to Point B. If you want to shortcut the scenic parts, why not walk through Florida by road? Better yet, why not skip the walking entirely and drive as fast as you can through the state?

A heron hunted in the sandy shallows of the outflow of Orlando Wetlands Park, not knowing this was the Magic City's effluent, treated of course. Cattail marshes centered the marshland. Buzzards gathered by the hundreds in the trees and along the marsh dike, warming in the morning sun.

A road walk led me north out of Orange County, where I was creeping into suburbia as suburbia was creeping into rural districts. A few orange groves and cow pastures were still hanging on. At the Seminole County line, a kiosk and trail marker hailed the arrival of the FT, which now joined the county's greenway system, spurring me on. This greenway was part of the Seminole Flagler Trail, which led past Lake Mills County Park. The path entered the former logging-town-turned-ghost-town-turned-Orlando-suburb of Chuluota. I followed the blazes closely here as the trail wound through streets and even along a power line right-of-way until emerging on Snow Hill Road, where the FT shortly began following an old railroad grade. In places, the grade was elevated far above a thick, deep swamp, where the water was covered in lime green duck moss. Deciduous trees were sporting the tiniest of leaves, beginning their transformation to summer green.

The FT did well following this grade, and the setting was a pleasant surprise as the path made its way around the northeast side of Orlando. The grade ran due north, into the Little Big Econ State Forest. Here, the FT bridged the Econlockhatchee River, parallel to the old railroad bridge. I turned west along the dark, sand-lined river, heading upstream, working around river meanders and over small bridges spanning deep gullies and old oxbows. At times, the FT ran on the river's edge, availing views of the sandbars. Turtles lounged in the sun. The Econ can get busy on nice weekends, with a large population living nearby. It was great for canoeing—I'd been down it myself.

In these parts I was seeing some new trees, indicating a change in climate and situation, the inexorable shifts of a trek north. Sweetgum, cedar, and magnolia dotted the woods. I found a campsite back from the river and out of the charging north wind. The night would be another cold one. The rollercoaster wasn't rising yet. Nights at campsites have their own ways of passing fast or slowly. It depends on how cold you are, how tired you are, and on other factors, like rain, wind, and company. The cold was here, but so was the fire, which I fed at times during the night, using wood placed within reach of the sleeping bag. I call this keeping an Indian fire. Indians chided white arrivals for making roaring fires hot enough to warp iron, yet too hot to get near. Later, when the fire died down, the white man was far away, requiring him to get out from beneath his blanket to rekindle it; Indians made a small fire, easy to stay near and easier to feed.

The trail then entered Oviedo, another Orlando suburb, in Seminole County.

A dense fog hung over the Econ as I left at first light. The track took good advantage of the Econ State Forest, staying within its bounds as long as possible before entering urban environs. Soon the morning work bell was ringing. Backhoes, trucks backing up, jackhammers, and other working sounds were drifting in as I left the Econ forest.

The trail then entered Oviedo, another Orlando suburb, in Seminole County. Through the town the trail went, using every creative technique in the book to keep the trail as much of a trail as possible. It followed a power line right-of-way. It traveled a boardwalk through a city park and ran along an abandoned railroad grade in the middle of town. It cut through a swamp, traversing a wooded no-man's-land. At times it crossed major roads and went along subdivisions, but I take my hat off to the Florida Trail Association here for doing well with what the setting offers.

Just beyond a busy intersection, the FT joined the Cross Seminole Trail, a paved multi-use greenway, tracing another old railroad grade. The level path was marked and paved and advertised itself as being part of the Florida Trail, with square posts emblazoned with the FT logo. Old runners, young bikers, dogs walking their people on tightly stretched leashes, hip roller-bladers, and a lone backpacker walking the length of Florida were all on the greenway. One woman was pushing her plush pooch in a baby stroller! The Florida Trail is unique in many aspects.

After six or seven miles, including a couple of creek spans on bridges, the bike path ended, and the trail entered a light industrial area, then seemingly dead-ended. I circled around, considering going into a business to inquire where the trail was; but real men are too embarrassed to ask for directions, especially hiking directions, and especially if they write hiking guidebooks for a living. As in the hurricane deadfall of Big Cypress, I kept scouting until I found the next orange blaze. The FT jigged through woods and sauntered to a power line right-of-way. Just as I was getting in tune with hiking beneath the metal towers, the FT changed again, entering Spring Hammock Park. The magnolia-dominated woods were thick, beautiful, and full of nature's rounded shapes, contrasting with the straight lines of the power grid. As I was becoming accustomed to the dense woods, the trail crossed a live railroad track and a road and then entered Soldier Creek Park. The costume changes were coming faster than a girl trying on outfits before a big party.

I walked along Soldier Creek, where the trail rolled up and down "moguls," small hills along the fast-moving, woodsy and attractive creek. I didn't know what to expect of the next leg. It proved to be a short road walk leading past Big Tree Park, where a sign proclaimed that this is where the world's largest cypress tree stands. A good place for a lunch break of peanut butter and spreadable fruit on tortilla bread, I figured. Black-clad motor bikers, tourists who follow trees, and working folk on their lunch break rolled into the park, taking the little path to the Big Tree. Then I was off again, as the FT joined another urban trail, this one the Rhinehart Road/Crossings Bike Path. It followed a huge power line also, entering full-blown suburbia in the town of Lake Mary. Stores and parking lots and traffic lights clogged the horizon. Traffic whizzed by.

More interesting, the first hills of the Florida Trail were ahead. Vertical variation! I waited at traffic lights after pushing the crossing button. I was glad to be a backpacking spectacle rather than a traffic-jammed driver behind the wheel. Where the sidewalk crossed business entrances, it had stop signs, quite unusual for a "trail." A plus for this path: trailside fountains. I would think about that when I grew thirsty on later trail segments. Having noted the definite dearth of campsites in these parts, I had arranged for another pickup by Aaron. This time we would drive to his parents' home in Lake County.

The highlight of this section was crossing Interstate 4 on a $3.6 million suspension bridge built strictly for the self-propelled travelers who used the greenway, which now left the power line and connected to the Seminole-Wekiva Bike Path. This track followed an old railroad grade heading west, the old Sanford Lake Eustis Railroad, completed in 1887. I called Aaron, and he picked me up where the rail trail crossed Orange Avenue.

Aaron's dad, Mike, greeted us at the door and immediately made me feel at home. Mike was a little older than I am and made a living as a remodeler, working for himself. His work kept him in good shape. Mike pointed me to the shower and I cleaned up, a necessary venture now that I was among clean people after this twenty-one-mile day. Aaron's mom, Judy, came in shortly thereafter. She and Mike were from Michigan. Their family exuded a positive, relaxed atmosphere, and I appreciated that. I also appreciated the steaks Mike cooked and the sides aplenty that Judy prepared. I stuffed myself. A backpacker's fare leads to such overindulgences, but the Marables understood. Later we went out to see two huge murals Aaron had recently completed at a house in Mount Dora. Aaron grew a notch more animated as he discussed the murals. His talent showed in his work, and we were all proud of his making the transition to full-time artist. Aaron

I asked Aaron to pose for a picture before I proceeded on down the Seminole-Wekiva Bike Path.

was doing what he loved, what he was passionate about, and he was getting paid for it: a dream job. I knew one when I saw it, for I have a dream job too, getting paid to hike, camp, and paddle all over this beautiful country. Additional perks of my dream job are being lost, cold, alone, wet, broke, hungry, thirsty, hot, sore, and dirty—all perfect qualifications for hiking the Florida Trail.

The next morning Mike, Aaron, and I ate breakfast at a nearby homespun eatery. When it was time to hit the trail, after a resupply, Aaron dropped me off back at Orange Avenue. I asked him to pose for a picture before I proceeded on down the Seminole-Wekiva Bike Path with an overloaded pack. This area was used to loads, I thought, as it once was the location of the Umatilla Fruit Company, which shipped its pickings on the old railroad that the bike path now followed. The weight of my backpack and the noncushiony paved trail combined to strain my feet; I was paying the price for my shoes' lightness and ability to drain and dry when wet. My feet were being taxed to the maximum, and the stress was troublesome.

Where the rail trail ended, I carefully road walked busy State Road 46 to cross the Wekiva River. Just ahead, the Seminole State Forest marked the end of the Orlando suburban walk. Thanks for sticking with me through the detail of rail trails, bike paths, and greenways; it may seem confusing on paper, but the routes on the ground were not hard to follow except at the one point mentioned, and neither was I put out that the trail was not wilder. Actually, I was amazed at the resourcefulness of the Florida trail Association in achieving a complete route.

Nonetheless, getting back into the woods felt good. My feet were much happier to be walking on a softer foot trail, especially with less than a mile to go to complete the six-mile day. Part of my newfound weight gain was an edited manuscript of *A Falcon Guide to Mammoth Cave National Park*, which I had completed in the fall. I was now to review the editorial changes. The package, picked up at the Marables' house, weighed 5 pounds, 2 ounces, according to the shipping label. This and ten days' worth of supplies made for a heavy pack. And I was stuck with the manuscript pages for a while, because I could neither eat nor drink them, nor burn them or throw them away.

I reached a ten-by-twenty-foot trail shelter with a tin roof and an open front facing south. This was home for the night as a major rain-bearing front was coming southward. We had looked at radar of the storm back at the Marables' place. It was wide and colorful. The coldest air of the season was to follow the front. For now the air was hot, though the dark front was already visible on the horizon. I unloaded the overloaded pack, sat down relieved, then went for water from a creek a quarter mile back. I settled in and waited for the rain. It came mixed with wind gusts and increasingly cool air. By dark I was clad in four layers, grateful for the water- and wind-blocking shelter. I lay in the bag that night listening to the off-again on-again rain patter on the tin roof. The lights of greater Orlando glowed to the south. I was glad to have the city behind me.

10

Sharks' Teeth and Shortcuts

The dark windy morning gave way to sunshine, but the air never reached the sixties, though it seemed the wind gusts were reaching the sixties, as in miles per hour. My feet appreciated the soft earth of the FT here, as it traversed gallberry-palmetto plains broken by pine woods featuring more sand pine and scrub oaks as I went north.

In five miles I reached a designated campsite known as Shark Tooth Spring. Backpackers were supposed to stay in designated sites in the state forests. On a hillside—yes, a hillside—ever-so-slightly sulphurous water emerged from a small rock opening, gurgling crystalline over gravel bordered by palms and ferns. The water tasted quite pleasant and was a major reason to be camping here. The spring was named for its propensity to spit out fossilized sharks' teeth from the cave opening.

The heavy weight of my pack spurred me to rummage for and expel every nonessential item in it. I found a bouillon cube, wrapped in gold foil. Hans had given it to me 350 miles before, back in the Big Cypress. It had been disappearing and reappearing in various pack pockets, as if it had legs. I decided to end its existence there and then. That would be a half-ounce loss of weight, too. After retrieving water from the spring, I boiled it up, poured the steaming liquid into my cup, and threw in the cube, watching it melt. The drink warmed me as the temperature plummeted that night.

The campsite location led to a sleeping dilemma. I could sleep by the metal campsite fire ring, but it was in an open grassy spot, exposed to the wind and frost. I could sleep back in the palmy woods, protected from the wind and frost, but then I wouldn't be near the heat of

Shark Tooth Spring gurgled crystalline over gravel bordered by palms and ferns.

the fire. I chose to sleep by the fire ring, later awaking to ground frost shimmering under an almost full moon. Out of wood, I jumped out of the bag and did the firewood-gathering-chill-dance by the light of overhead orb, crunching frost with each step, then reignited the fire and cinched the bag tighter to cut the breeze blowing on the back of my neck. I surmised that the bears of Seminole State Forest were quite happy that night to have a thick coat of hair. This locale featured some of the Sunshine State's thickest black bear populations. The wilder the better, I say. When a wild animal as far up the food chain as a black bear can thrive, that means everything below it has a refuge, too, in the "real natural Florida," to quote the Florida State Parks motto, part of what the Florida Trail is about.

The chilly morn hadn't warmed by the time I spanned Sulphur Run and later left the state forest. A little road walk soon led me through a mix of houses and state forest land. I was making great time along State Road 44, moving to stay warm, when I hit a snag.

The gravel road I was on continued forward, but orange blazes entered the woods, heading left and right, north and south. I took the south path, tracing faint blazes into woods dense with saw palmetto and fallen sand pines. Within moments I was crawling and climbing, having to snap off tree limbs and tear through arm-grabbing vines, and I hit a wet area with a broken-down bridge. I sloshed in above my shoe tops. Wet, cold feet.

Ahead were more blowdowns, so thick that I decided to detour. These were fallen sand pines, with stiff limbs that could scratch through clothes. I made my way to the edge of a pond. Can you imagine fallen trees forming such a barricade that you decide walking through a pond on a cold morning is a better option? That little trick led to thigh-deep water, and then returning to the trail was difficult with the fallen pines so dense. Finally, I bashed back into the woods and found the trail. After more wrangling, it opened to what looked like a defunct church camp, with outbuildings and such. The blazes continued along a power line, splitting two ponds. Beyond the ponds, the trail blazes disappeared. I continued tracing the power line.

Road noise ahead. I was back at SR 44, where I had earlier been road walking. It became obvious that I'd been following an abandoned segment of the FT. What to do now? What is one to do when the writer of hiking guidebooks can't follow a trail? The last thing I wanted to do was go back through that overgrown, blown down briery or wet hell, or repeat the road walk. The only thing worse than backtracking to where you started was to backtrack to where you started backtracking in the first place. Anyway, to backtrack is to admit defeat—I would devise a shortcut and intersect the Florida Trail! I backtracked just a little, coming to a fence line, which I followed westward until it met a transmission line of some sort, still going west. Follow that and meet the Florida Trail, I thought. Simple. Tracing the cleared transmission line right-of-way went well, and the already sunny day got a little brighter—until the transmission line led into a swamp.

I stubbornly plunged into the swamp, clinging to the plan as a drowning man clutches a life preserver. The aqua, clogged with stringy tentacle-like waterweeds, soon reached up to my crotch. The swamp went as far as I could see. Damn the water—full speed ahead. And I powered on as fast as the uneven swamp floor would allow. The plan began to seem like a bad idea, then a ridiculous one. I looked around, wondering how and why I had gotten myself here. I'd committed Outdoor Mistake No. 1: get lost, then try to find a new way out rather than backtracking to the last known spot and orienting from there.

Admitting my mistake, I ashamedly backtracked again to a road-bed leading north. This I followed, dripping swamp water and wearing water weeds for leg decorations. The roadbed ran into freshly painted blazes of the FT! The trail! I persuaded myself that the plan had worked, give or take a few kinks along the way. The funny thing was that this trail section would itself soon be abandoned for a reroute through pure woods of Lake Norris Conservation Area. Anticipating this was part of why I had kept following the faint blazes through the overgrown blowdown area. I had speculated that recent hurricane damage coupled with lack of maintenance due to the impending re-route had left the trail in its poor state. Incorrect surmises.

I was wet, cut up, and worn out but nevertheless determined to complete the planned fourteen-mile day. I proceeded on, Lewis and Clark style, eventually making the Winn-Dixie Boy Scout Reservation, through which the FT ran. Scouting officials allowed thru-hiker camping. The sun was still high enough to warm me, so I sat in the sun of a field and dried my shoes and socks (off), and pants (on), wondering if I could turn the waterweeds into a salad. The sun sank behind a line of trees, and I made camp under a big live oak. The live oak canopy would minimize frost and provide shelter from the wind, too. Also, wood was abundant. The weather radio was calling for temps to drop into the twenties, bringing the "coldest day in three years." Indeed, I was warmer that night than the night before due to this wind and frost protection as well as through making a long, narrow fire along which I lay, with a fresh stock of broken oak to make it through the night.

Even while entirely cinched in the bag, like a butterfly in a cocoon, you can sense the progress of a restoked fire. First, the firelight shines through the bag, then the heat penetrates the layers of insulation. Then you begin to wonder if you have put on too much wood, as the side of you closest to the fire becomes a tad too warm. Is the sleeping bag melting? You vow to stay awake through the apex of the fire. But the warmth makes an already drowsy man unable to stay awake, and you comfortably slumber once again. Sure enough, it went down to 21 degrees. The scout reservation spigot was frozen in the morning, so I doused the fire with water from the nearby pond, then crunched across the frozen ground, amid frost-encrusted palmettos glittering in the morning sun. Before long I reached a Florida Trail milestone—the Ocala National Forest, and Clearwater Lake Campground. I was at the spot where Jim Kern, the founder of the Florida Trail, had painted the first blazes marking the route.

I sat in the chilly shade of the campground trailhead, waiting to meet Ken ReCorr, reporter for the Ocala newspaper. An ex-New Yorker-via-North Carolina, he was doing a story on my trek. As I waited, up came the heavily clad host of Clearwater Lake Campground, Larry Bates, in a golf cart. We visited a while, and the sixty-year-old northeasterner concluded his visit by asking if I wanted some coffee to warm up. A few minutes later he showed up with a full pot, milk, honey, and an oatmeal breakfast. No matter how bad this oatmeal was, I told myself, I had to finish it. But this was real oatmeal, with freshly cut apples and raisins. How nice of him! I remarked on the difference between real oatmeal and the packaged gagmeal I'd been eating. And I had no trouble finishing off the breakfast and thanking Larry for his kindness.

Then the reporter arrived. Ken was wearing a knit cap and layers of clothing. The chill was getting to everyone. A photographer joined him, and we worked on the story for a couple of hours. He interviewed Larry the campground host as well. I mentioned that Larry was just one of many people who had bent over backwards in kindness to this wandering FT backpacker. Ken asked me about the biggest surprise of the trip thus far, and I said that was it: how pleasant and helpful so many strangers had been. After Ken and the pho-

I crunched across the frozen ground amid frost-encrusted palmettos glittering in the morning sun.

tographer left, and I sat down again to relax, a small white sedan came driving right up at me in the trailhead parking lot. The driver opened the door and asked, "Are you a Florida Trail thru-hiker?" Apparently I had the thru-hiker look. Did this mean I exuded a trail-savvy aura? Or was it just that I looked grubby and haggard, like a guy living on two changes of clothing?

The question asker introduced himself as Jon Phipps. What coincidence! We had e-mailed a few times before my hike—I had asked him for some trail advice. Jon offered to help and took me to the post office, where I mailed off the reviewed manuscript of the Mammoth Cave book. That took five pounds off my back. We returned to the trailhead and Jon Phipps went on his own hike, while I waited for Jeff Cochran, one of the fabulous firemen from South Florida. What a busy, sociable morning for a lone hiker accustomed now to solitude. Jeff was to join me for the sixty-five-mile trek through the Ocala National Forest.

11

The Scrubby Sea

Jeff arrived about 2:30 and we were soon walking north on the Florida Trail, following the FT's first blazes through slanted pines, buffeted by a dying wind. We were hitting it hard, making a fast pace to beat the sunset, but it wasn't necessary as we made the 5.2 miles well before dark. I retrieved water from a nearby stream, toting it to a level forested campsite. I readied the camp with wood in preparation for another cold night. Jeff surprised me with some bratwurst that we cooked. If an army travels on its stomach, so does a hiker. Food becomes a bigger matter on the trail than in ordinary life because you have what is in your pack, and that's it. A package of hot chocolate becomes a fine dessert, whereas in town, if you don't have enough food in the larder at home, you can always go to the store or a restaurant to fill up.

The water-filled pot showed a skim of ice the next morning. Jeff, despite his West Virginia roots, was now a full-blown short-pants-wearin' South Floridian and seemed surprised at the chill. We dashed around breaking camp and set out, crossing a series of boardwalks bisecting a swamp where I noticed large bay trees growing. They say winter in Florida is over by 10:00 a.m., and it wasn't long before we were wishing for shade. But the scenery was nothing short of grand as we passed through pine savannas, scrub oak forests, and sand pine scrub.

"I didn't know you were going to take me to the mountains," joked Jeff as we scaled numerous hills, which added more beauty to the area. In fact, we surmounted 100 feet in elevation, according to the GPS I was using to remeasure sections of the FT for the second edition of *The Hiking Trails of Florida's National Forests, Parks, and Preserves.* I took notes with the same digital recorder I was using for this book.

The thirteen-mile day landed us near Farles Prairie Campground, where we could camp in the backcountry yet enjoy access to water from the campground pitcher pump. The afternoon was positively balmy, and I joyfully went sockless while leaning against my backpack, which was leaning against a leaning sand pine. It might have been pleasant to have had a lounge chair to enhance my comfort, but I thought of all the people in lounge chairs at the moment, not having exercised and smelling clean and consuming food and drink from well-stocked cupboards. I envisioned myself in later life, in good health and good shape, quite comfortable, while those who had chosen the easy life might face pain and health dilemmas. You never know, of course, but it seemed my life of exercise in the outdoors might give me the last laugh while others are waiting for the magic pill. I hear people grousing about the cost of health care all the time, yet they don't take care of their own health. Anything worth having, like good health, does not come easy. The Johnny Molloy Health Plan is simple and cheap—walk to live, keep moving now to keep moving later.

This was positively the last night that was going to get cold, according to the weather radio—until the next front. The temperature dipped into the thirties. Both Jeff and I slept out under the trees and stars, sprawled in front of the crackling sand pine fire. Another chilly start kept us moving as we passed along the rim of Farles Prairie. The sandhill cranes were up early too, echoing their unique chortle across the clearings. The water of the interconnected ponds comprising Farles Prairie was the highest in years, and the added aqua added to the charm of the landscape. The water and grass prairies extended to far lines of trees, while up close, live oak hammocks and longleaf pines bordered the trail. Often a ring of sand bordered the ponds and upon the sand the trail traveled, tracing the margin between water and trees, winding along the shore of the wetlands, curving with their convolutions.

As we rounded a bend, a thin gray man in his sixties appeared, carrying a backpack festooned with many water bottles. He was happy to see us and repeatedly said so, talking and talking and talking, eyes flailing about as quickly as he was changing subjects. The solitude was apparently getting to him. Bug Eyes talked of campsites, weather, fasting, water, and everything else, especially the "Rainbow People" who hung out in the Ocala National Forest. The Rainbow People call themselves the "largest non-organization of non-members in the world." I think of them as a band of dropouts, people who shun "the system," preferring their own way of life, which to me appeared like a lot of partying and very little working. They claim to have a close connection to the earth, but if you have seen their campsites, and I have seen many of them, you might conclude that you were looking at a bunch of slobs and litterbugs who just like to laze around the woods.

The Rainbow People are anticommercial and not aligned with any political movement. Most proclaim themselves hippies and say their gatherings are just assemblies of people practicing peace. Large numbers of Rainbow People wintered here, occasionally working at temporary jobs in the town of Ocala. I had spent a considerable amount of time in the Ocala year after year, had seen plenty of them, and knew that the Rainbows had provoked hostilities in local towns, especially Salt Springs, where merchants allowed only a few people in a store at a time to minimize theft. The Rainbow People use national forests all over the United States to hold annual summer gatherings. Ask a Rainbow person what they are about, and you will get a very different picture than what I have described. They are the stuff of legend in the Ocala. Jeff kept hoping we would run into a clan.

We gave Bug Eyes his solitude back and proceeded on. Ponds were rimmed in tan grasses and sand, from which rose forth a line of longleaf pines. On higher terrain grew canopies of live oaks, under which scrub oaks and palmetto competed for ground space. I enjoyed walking where live oak limbs arched overhead, as they gave the forest a fairyland appearance. The bears loved the live oaks and the acorns they dropped. We came upon a large and fresh pile of bear poop, and began seeing tracks along the sandy trail. The bear was a big one, judging by its prints in the sand. We hoped to see it, but it stayed out of our sight. The evergreen live oaks and pines and the sylvan understory were pleasing on the eye; the forests I had left behind in East Tennessee's mountains were still cloaked in the drab browns and grays of leafless winter, with occasional coats of white.

After several miles along Farles, the trail turned away from the prairie and its windings to head north into a mature sand pine forest of what I call the Florida Hill Country. The swales and crests were covered in tall sand pine, each tree with its own distinct lean, never growing straight for the sky, their needle-topped apexes gathering like the heads of drunken tree-men, hanging on to one another for support. The sun played a role in the illusion, its light deflected by the thousands of tilted evergreens. Sometimes sunrays made it to the forest floor, sometimes not. Deer moss, a lime green and gray lichen spread on the forest floor, added color distinction. When dry, as deer moss usually was, it would crumble to dust at a footstep, but after a rain it would flatten like a sponge at your passing and then sprang back as if you were never there. Deer moss grew profusely among the hilly sand pines. The pines' small, hard and tight cones gave no quarter at our feet, holding strong like rocks on a mountain footpath. Jeff and I carefully placed our feet away from the cones, occasionally kicking them away, lest we slip on them.

A woodpecker chuckled in the distance. Beyond the sand pines I walked in a trance, feet in one place, mind in another, and was startled when a bunch of wild turkeys in the trees overhead squawked their departure. It's funny what happens when you hike. Your mind wanders too. Sometimes it is where you are, and you think about your immediate environment, or a need, like water. Sometimes your thoughts are a million miles away from the trail, thinking about the four-year-old kid down the block, when you were four also, who intentionally scuffed his new white buckle-topped leather shoes so that he wouldn't have to wear them to Sunday School. You may drift back to a fourth grade spelling bee when you won the contest, only to lose on the very first word when placed in competition with the fifth and sixth grade winners of the elementary school championship. Or your mind may revisit a place where you once were, and how the cabin smelled of old rich wood and the light aroma of ashes from the wood stove, or it may come upon a funny or fascinating a story in your life that deserves retelling to yourself. If the hike is long, you try to flesh out every detail of the story. And perhaps you even laugh out loud, scaring a turkey in turn.

But sooner or later the focus always comes back to the trail, where the feet proceed forward, and the eyes scan for the proper places for each footfall. Then you notice the shape of a tree, or the color of a plant, or the angle of sunlight in a sand pine forest, and if you are a writer, you may write about it.

The hum of State Road 40 brought me away from such musings. The Florida Trail crossed it ahead. Spindly young sand pines grew so densely and close to the trail as to eliminate the margin of error for a hiker. With a dip of elevation, the scenery changed. We spanned a boardwalk in a moist palm forest, crossed the busy state road, and immediately retreated into the woods again, turning west. Ahead the forest gave way and we opened onto an area where the timber had been cut, revealing naked undulating hills and valleys. Tree rubble left over from the harvest lay in a thin sheet over the rolling land. A trailside sign erected by the U.S. Forest Service explained that Hurricanes Jeanne and Francis had downed a lot of mature sand pines, and a mop-up timbering operation had followed. The area now was open to the sun, and the day promptly lost its cool.

I understood the salvage timbering. The sand pine is a short-lived tree by any standard; a century-old sand pine is ancient. These pines were already on their last legs before the hurricanes hit. Now the Forest Service could harvest and replant the pines, using best forest management practices. The landscape that looked so naked would be clothed again, although perhaps not fully clothed within the span of our lifetimes. We tend to define changes within the short perspective of our own lives, ignoring Mother Nature's longer spans.

We stopped at the Juniper Prairie campground entrance road just ahead, filling our bottles from a spigot, then moved on into the Juniper Prairie Wilderness. A sign warned of a more challenging path. This wilderness is managed differently than other areas of the forest and is more subject to fire. This has resulted in a stunted short forest in places, leaving the sandy trailbed open to the sun. Luckily for us, clouds scudded in, delivering shade. The trailside sand made the trail loose, slowing down two hot and fatigued backpackers. I tried to raise our spirits by promising a stream to swim and big oaks for shade ahead. We proceeded on, passing ponds and some dense thickets of young spindly sand pines, making the trail so narrow that tree limbs caught our packs.

Whispering Creek was high, like all the forest's waters, and we danced across it on a narrow log. From here we trudged the last mile to Whiskey Creek and a campsite in low-slung sand live oaks. But I had been enticing Jeff with the attributes of Juniper Creek, with its cool waters and big oaks. "It's only an eighth of a mile farther," I said, not adding the words "off trail." We bashed through the brush, which featured fallen trees aplenty, courtesy of the hurricanes. Brambles and briers grew in the clearings left by fallen trees. I had done this before and on that occasion had found a nice site under wide-spreading live oak directly beside the creek. Juniper Creek is a swift, clear stream fed by a massive spring and is one of Florida's finest canoeing destinations.

This time, however, we were trying for Juniper Creek by a different route, and our ramblings led us into palmy jungle with spongy, uneven soil unfit even for a rest break. I raised the white flag. We turned back to the long-used campsite fifty yards north of Whiskey Creek. "Nothing like some woods bashing to end the day," I laughed to Jeff. He rolled his eyes and dumped his pack. We lay around the campsite, enjoying the nonmovement and lack of packs on our backs, living out what I call the Twenty-Foot Radius Theory. After dropping that pack at camp, a tired hiker will not go farther than twenty feet from the stopping point unless absolutely necessary.

The evening was much warmer than the previous one, and Jeff made a fire for cooking and atmosphere, rather than purely for warmth. The next morning dawned cool and foggy. We made the most of the morning cool, winding through rolling sand pine and sand live oak thickets. Dead tree snags rose above the vaporous swales. The morning sun rapidly dissipated the fog as we arrived at Hidden Pond. This is perhaps the most heavily used campsite on the entire Florida Trail, which was why we avoided it, even on a weekday. The pond is attractive and is truly hidden among the high hills of the Juniper Prairie Wilderness.

More pond prairies bordered the trail ahead, where Jeff and I pushed through head-high wiregrass. Where their edges were devoid of the grasses, the still waters reflected the forests beside them. Some ponds were more grass than water; others were covered with lily pads. Climbing a large hill brought us to the edge of Pats Island and a line of old and impressive live oaks. Here in the Ocala National Forest, the term *island* was used to describe areas of fertile soil dominated by oaks and longleaf pines encircled by less fertile sand pine scrub. These settlers were literally in a scrubby sea, and the Ocala National Forest still preserves the largest sand pine scrub forest on the planet. In days long past, settlers homesteaded on these "islands," growing crops and living off the land. Pats Island is easily the most famous thanks to the book *The Yearling*, which was made into a movie starring Gregory Peck and filmed on site. Author Marjorie Kinnan Rawlings stayed with the last two residents of Pats Island, Calvin and Mary Long, which gave her book great authenticity, capturing the lives of these early Florida pioneers. Pats Island was abandoned for good in 1935.

On Pats Island the forest transitioned to longleaf pine. The needles were so thick in places as to prevent any growth on the forest floor, a bronze base from which rose large-trunked pines topped with splaying green-tipped branches. We left the Juniper Prairie Wilderness at Forest Road 10, aiming north for Hopkins Prairie. Suddenly the trail veered off into thick woods, away from the waters of the prairie, which were not normally near the trail here. I crossed the forest road leading to Hopkins Prairie Campground and found the road underwater near the trail crossing. Uh-oh. The forest road showed no auto tracks either. Hopkins Prairie Campground should have been open at this season, but we arrived to find it closed due to high water.

I sat still, perusing the trail map, then "proceeded on."

The trail took us to the edge of the campground and we took a break. Jeff went to fill our bottles from the campground pump well, having to work around a flooded part of the road. The picture spelled trouble for us, as the FT circled the edge of Hopkins Prairie for the next four plus miles, traveling between the prairie and the flanking live oak woods. After perusing the trail map, we proceeded on. Just a few yards of walking and we were into the water.

Thus began the longest water slog since the Big Cypress, where Jeff had also been my companion in swamp walking. But this time it was completely unexpected. Hurricanes had dumped excessive water the previous season, and the water had yet to drain off fully. Depths ranged from thigh deep to ankle deep over the next four miles, which also included a few dry spots—just enough to get our hopes up that the water walk would end, and then back into the drink we went. In my five previous walkings of the Florida Trail segment through the Ocala, Hopkins Prairie had never even been close to being flooded, but flooded it was. Brush grew thick along the path. In places, we had

Thus began the longest water slog since the Big Cypress, where Jeff had also enjoyed swamp walking.

to detour around fallen trees on an inundated track, doubling our challenge. At least the footing was better here on the sandy lake bottom rather than the eroded limestone of the Big Cypress. But a lot of gunk grew in the shallowest waters. Minnows darted from my path above sunken pine needles. A rim of pollen lay along the shoreline, showing that the water had been a good foot higher than it was now. Our pace dropped by half, but we enjoyed the solitude. The swamp slog killed our wildlife viewing opportunities. The sound of legs striding through water carries a long way and irritates even the hiker after a while: *slosh, slosh, slosh, slosh.*

The deepest water was at the end of the prairie. I had to pull the contents from my pants pockets to keep them dry. I scared off two largemouth bass in this deep section. One good aspect: walking through the water like this defined the true meaning of "wash and wear." The FT finally left flooded Hopkins Prairie and led over wooded sand pine hills to the junction with the Salt Springs Spur Trail. The strange part of the hike became the silence of dry land trail hiking. My ears had gotten used to the sloshing.

This spur path led to the actual Salt Springs and the hamlet of Salt Springs. However, we took it but a quarter mile to a pond I knew. The pond was next to a first-rate campsite beneath tall longleaf pines, wide-spreading oaks, and a cushiony forest floor of nothing but pine needles. We made the quarter mile and reached the unnamed pond, now more of a lake, far higher than I had ever seen it. The campsite was within view, but to reach it we had to walk the grassy lake edge because the thick forest prevented access any other way. We reluctantly stepped in and walked the lake's edge, wondering which step would take us deeper than already thigh-deep water. The final slog was much harder here than back at Hopkins Prairie. The pond floor was not compacted since we were not on a trail, and the pond grass grew thick. I observed that yesterday we had ended our hike with an off-trail ramble, and today we were ending with an extra wading session. Jeff openly questioned the wisdom of joining me in the Ocala. I think he was joking.

Dry land felt mighty good. The campsite was as appealing as ever, rewarding us for our efforts. Collecting water for camp required one more thigh-deep trip into the lake to reach clear open water, as the immediate shoreline was grassy and covered in waterweeds, but then we jumped into the drying process, hoping for no more wet surprises. The two of us passed the mild evening before a crackling pine fire. Just as we retired, the moon rose between the pines, forcing me to cover my eyes with a bandana tied around my head. We were out on a point, nearly encircled by water, including another pond nearby. The frogs were staging an amphibian musical all around us, drowning out even the usual evening bugs. They croaked in time, rising to a crescendo, then fell off, then rose again. Others sang their own songs. It was a much richer lullaby than those sleep tapes people play, mimicking oceans waves and the like. This was the real thing. Jeff offered that the frogs might be laughing at us for trying to operate in their watery world.

The sun was just rising over the unnamed pond as we repeated our wade to return to the Salt Springs Trail. The difference was that the temperature was 50 degrees instead of 75! Once back on dry land, I put on my socks and squished uptrail with numbed feet to rejoin the Florida Trail. From here we pounded forth, soon reaching a pine savanna. Longleaf pines towering over wiregrass formed layers of color. At the lowest level, the tan wiregrass, resembling amber waves of grain, spread wide to the horizon. Above that, brown and black pine trunks rose vertically to a green layer of uniform height, starting about forty feet up. Iridescent green needles spread a gently feathered canopy, with the needles of one tree nearly—but not quite—touching the next. Above that arched the rich blue sky of a Florida winter. The layers of color rose and fell with the rolling terrain, where wide and shallow sinkholes were also covered in this longleaf-wiregrass assemblage that once grew 90 million acres strong across the Southeast. The ecosystem was simple, open, and dependent on fires to keep it that way. Purple violets, tiny yet vivid, and literally few and far between, offered another tint to the woodland.

Sand roads divided the longleaf forest from the more predominant sand pine forest. These sand roads allowed the Forest Service to manage the two ecosystems each according to their needs. I understand that the roads had been cut at the dividing line between the ecosystems, but it didn't alter the strangeness of having radically differing forests just across the road from each other. I noticed on the GPS that these longleaf pine woods were the highest lands in all of the Ocala National Forest, soaring above 140 feet in elevation.

We crossed County Road 314. I stood still for a second, and a car pulled up, then stopped. I presumed someone was going to ask, "Are you a Florida Trail thru-hiker?" I wasn't expending any extra energy to walk to them; a woman going on sixty but dressed as if she was twenty emerged from the car and walked over to me. She said, "I'm lost. Do you know the way to Micanopy?" I did, and I explained directions. Question: Why would someone in a car pull over and ask a hiker for driving directions?

As 50 degrees became 72 degrees and we grew warm as we reached the side trail to the 88 Store, a half mile off the FT near Lake Kerr. We followed the blue-blazed spur path leading to the country store and bar. I changed my disgusting hiking shirt for a cleaner one before entering the business, then laid my pack by a pinball machine. Near us, a few racks held limited dry goods such as chips. A glass wall cooler with beer and soft drinks glowed fluorescently. The other two thirds of the otherwise dark room had Formica tables and plastic-covered seats and smelled like a bar. An overhead light illuminated the pool table. Beer signs adorned the walls. Black plastic-pad-topped bar stools bellied up to the bar.

The matron, quite friendly, welcomed us. The 88 Store was well acquainted with hikers; there was even a trail register sitting on the bar for hikers to sign. This was likely the most perused trail register on the Florida Trail. Most others were at remote trailheads, often some distance back in the woods to prevent vandalism. Jeff turned the corner near the beer and saw what we were looking for: hot dogs. Against the back wall in this nook was chili. I asked if they had bread, and the woman pointed to the bottom of the dry goods rack. Buns. The package was complete. We grabbed a few more snacks and other assorted fare unavailable in our packs and moseyed on out to the covered porch. I sat under a NASCAR race schedule, slugging a two-liter cooler-chilled Diet Coke directly from the jug. Enjoying the slight breeze that wafted onto the porch, we watched customers come and go. Ah, the world was ours. Jeff waxed eloquent and elaborate, planning his next Ocala hike to stop here, where he could camp in the woods behind the bar, then hang out among the neon signs in the evening, soaking up the atmosphere and a few cold ones, before stumbling back to the tent.

But not this time, as we had miles to go before a sober slumber. We hit the trail hard, trying to beat the heat, trekking the last two miles of a ten-mile day to reach Grassy Pond, formerly a campground but now merely a field bordered by woods. We made camp near the lake

Enjoying the slight breeze that wafted onto the porch at 88 Store, we watched customers come and go.

and made for the shade. The weather rollercoaster was rising high and fast. Since it was Saturday, ATVS, motorcyclists, and other hikers passed by.

Jeff did not realize how much he had missed backpacking. He had earlier trekked a lot up in my neck of the woods, the Southern Appalachians, and these last two trips had rekindled the desire in him. He spoke of future trips, future plans and new gear, what to take and what to leave behind. Things can go that way. Time, family commitments, and other ties that bind eat up your life. Hobbies and personal interests can fall by the wayside. Your nonfamily passions can drift away. Then years later an opportunity arises and the flame reignites. Jeff was carrying the torch again.

Our intolerance for discomfort also keeps us at home. We don't get cold because we don't have to, we don't cook over fires any more because we don't have to. We don't walk from one place to another because we don't have to. We sit in front of a television watching other people live on the small screen, perhaps now supplanted by a giant screen—other people actually doing the things that we find interesting. I call it voyeurism. We become spectators, sitting on life's sideline, voluntarily sitting on the bench, riding the pine and wondering why our own lives are unsatisfactory. Backpacking is an active, participative event, where you create and ultimately live out your own adventures. You're on the field, in the play; you have a uniform on, you're in the game.

Our world is much easier today; getting the simple necessities of life is straightforward. And with our excess time we invent psychoses and crises to fill the void. We hear about life being so stressful nowadays. Our ancestors' stresses were more immediate—keeping themselves warm, dry, and fed. Survival stresses are much more palpable than the stress of a long traffic-laden commute, or lack of life fulfillment, or cramming more into your schedule than you can realistically do. Backpacking simplifies your life and takes you back to taking care of the basics. It shows how few and simple our true needs are and how happy one can be simply by being dry and warm before a fire. Sharing a sense of accomplishment by walking twelve miles together with a friend or your family shows how simple happiness can be. It is the basic simplicity of backpacking that is its greatest offering in a world that we unnecessarily complicate.

We moved with the shade, making the most of a nice warm breeze blowing in from Grassy Pond. I took a much needed bath in Grassy Pond, stripping naked in the sun and washing myself and my clothes, then reviewed the editing of an article I had written for *Sea Kayaker* magazine. At Aaron's parents' house I had printed out the edited article from an e-mail. Jeff promised to mail off the marked-up copy to Seattle, where *Sea Kayaker* was based. The work bell never stops ringing when you work for yourself. As any self-employed person knows, the only time you waste on the job is your own, so when you work, you work hard, and you never work harder than when you work for yourself.

It was President's Day weekend, a busy outdoor weekend in Florida, with the extra day off. The forest was hopping. To my surprise, a group of ten or so backpackers walked up. Some scouts were already camping here. Later, another group came in, got water, and moved on. Grassy Pond was the only place to get water for several miles in either direction. At twilight, a lone backpacker pulled in for the night. This was one of only two campsites on the entire Florida Trail hike that I shared with other backpacking groups. A few mosquitoes joined the evening fire, and despite them and the possibility of rain, we camped out under the stars. I appreciated the warm night after several cold evenings. Around midnight, a light drizzle hit. I moved my bedding under a nearby live oak, whereas Jeff just pulled his plastic ground sheet over himself and slept on. We had lost the bet against a predicted 20 percent chance of rain. However, the misting rain shortly dissipated, after which the wind died and the mosquitoes were troublesome. I couldn't complain, since it had been many days since I'd had a bug problem. I was too lazy to put up the netting, instead covering most of my face with a bandana. Years of camping in less than perfect conditions allowed me to return to sleep easily.

Before dawn I awoke, the mosquitoes now nagging me more than the snooze button on an alarm clock. Jeff and I broke camp just as a second mist began to fall on us. The cloudy day continued to cool down as we pushed north through open pine forests in rolling woods. The undulating hills and swaying wiregrass resembled a gently rolling sea. The image was enhanced by the rolling hills. The wind picked up as we reached the northern end of the Ocala National Forest and Rodman Reservoir, which impounded the gorgeous Ocklawaha River. The lake moved angrily with waves driven by a biting cold wind that crashed into a shoreline littered with driftwood logs. A thick drizzle obscured the far side of the impoundment. The lakeshore shone, despite the weather, with its magnolias, water oaks, live oaks, and palms all draped in swaying Spanish moss, gracing the sandy shoreline.

Rodman Reservoir was part of the ill-fated Cross Florida Canal, intended to allow boat traffic to cut across the peninsula rather than going around it. First cooked up by the Spaniards, the idea had almost become a reality before it was killed for environmental reasons, and now the lands purchased for the canal constitute the Cross Florida Greenway, which the Florida Trail was to follow for a while.

Jeff and I had reached the outflow of Rodman Dam, where the Ocklawaha was unleashed to journey down to meet the St. Johns River. Mustachioed Dave, an old high school friend of Jeff's, sat clean and neat in his car, ready to shuttle Jeff back to his starting point and car. We said our goodbyes and off they went in the warm, dry automobile, likely to eat a fine lunch. I stood in the cold wet wind, briefly overcome with jealousy. I walked on, stopping later in a sheltered location for a modest lunch of tuna fish and pita bread. The day was dark and cold, then the trail became wet. When you got right down to it, I'd rather be tracing the FT to completion than sitting in a restaurant, but I had to remind myself of that every wet cold step forward.

The trail paralleled a paved road connecting Rodman Dam to State Road 19. Some middle-aged backpackers were going the other way on the road. They hailed me across a narrow strip of trees, one of the four asking, "How far are you going?" I replied proudly, "All the way." And he said, "To Maine?" Answer: "I think the Florida Trail ends in Florida." I was being a smart-ass. By "all the way" he thought I meant hiking the Florida Trail, then continuing through Alabama to meet the Pinhoti Trail, connecting with the Appalachian Trail, and following that all the way its conclusion in Maine. I considered hiking the Florida Trail an accomplishment in its own right, and his question inadvertently belittled this. I couldn't seem to win. Either people knew next to nothing about the Florida Trail, or else they knew enough to confound my growing sense of accomplishment.

Jeff and I had already made eleven miles before he left. I carried on, now officially on Cross Florida Greenway public lands. I donned my jacket despite the warmth built up from hiking. The previous day I had sought the breeze for cooling; today I avoided the breeze because it was too cool—rollercoaster down. My friend Bryan Delay calls it "playing the weather cards you are dealt." The Florida Trail now ascended the levee that ran above the barge canal, which was still active here, though it served only recreational boaters. Unlike the levees down south, this one was wooded along either side and atop the actual berm. The levee was irregular in height but offered a nice vantage and a soft grassy track that was pleasant on the feet. The actual canal, unoccupied in the sullen afternoon, ran to my left.

This eighteen-mile day brought me within striking distance of Buckman Lock, which had to be crossed during business hours. I was up bright and early the next morning, ready to cross the vestige of the grand water transportation scheme. I walked up to a gate, rang a buzzer, and waited in the cool mist. The lock tender came out of a little building and hollered, "It's unlocked." I sheepishly walked through the metal gate, having not even looked at the gate handle. The steel gangway was slippery as I spanned the canal boaters used to reach the St. Johns River.

After crossing SR 19 I left the Cross Florida Greenway and entered Plum Creek Timber property, signing the hiker register. I had seen no other northbound (or southbound) Florida Trail thru-hikers but knew some were several days ahead of me, because they had been signing the registers. While hiking the private timber tract I imagined these other hikers, what they looked like, and what stories they could tell. Their comments were short, limited to a sentence or two, usually remarking upon either beauty or weather when they went through. But we had traveled the same terrain and I had a story to tell. Surely so did they. This was wet, low-lying Florida I was walking through, much of it not quite land, yet not quite water either. The eroded roads were laid out in a grid built up using nearby soil from borrow pits to keep them from being so soggy.

The early morning trek through the private tract made the case for private landowners not allowing people to cross their land. All terrain vehicles had damaged the place, and it had also been used as an illegal dump. It had more refrigerators than your local Sears. When a private property owner allows public access, the owner is often the loser. Bad apples treat the place as though they don't own the place, because they don't, and in this unfortunate era of suing mania, liability is an issue. This place was abused. But I was grateful to Plum Creek, and presumably so is the Florida Trail Association, for allowing the FT to connect the trail between the Cross Florida Greenway and the Caravelle Ranch Wildlife Management Area, a public tract that limited use. Talk about a tale of two properties: upon entering Caravelle it was a different world. No eroded ATV tracks, no pot-holed forest roads, and no trash.

The mist ceased as the trail joined an old railroad grade, also built up in this wet woodland. I stopped and took a break where the trail crossed the old railroad bridge over a swamp-bordered creek. The stream waters were moving fast as I dipped in my water bottle and added instant tea mix, after which you couldn't tell a lick of difference in the color. It was tea-colored before the tea mix ever entered it. It didn't taste bad, though.

Rice Creek Sanctuary, another public tract, was north of the State Road 20 crossing. At first, the Florida Trail traced old logging roads, then it entered a gorgeous swamp, using Hoffman's Crossing, a wooden berm walkway nearly a third of a mile long. Think of the labor to make a bridge over 1,700 feet of swamp! Overhead, iron-wood trees, also known as hornbeam, were greening amid the lush swamp forest. Below, duck moss added more emerald color to this isle of beauty. This is the way of the Florida Trail: cross a road, follow a closed forest road, then *bam*, hit superlative splendor that displays scenery rivaling anything in America. Beyond the wooden walkway the trail meandered through more rich forests, with loblolly pine, oaks aplenty, palms, cypress, sweetgum, and bay trees rising forth from a brushy floor that was certainly underwater for some months of the year. The track was spongy, and wet in places, but it took me through a corridor of flora that shrieked, "Florida!" Now I knew why they call Rice Creek a sanctuary. The place was that beautiful. The contemplation bench built on the walkway was very appropriate.

A side trail over a raised soil berm led me to Oak Hammock camp-site. It gave that middle-of-nowhere feeling that I like in a campsite. The clouds broke shortly after my arrival and I whiled away the af-ternoon glad to spend President's Day in Rice Sanctuary. Rice Creek Swamp was the site of a rice and indigo plantation in the 1700s. The St. Johns Water Management District purchased over four thousand acres in 2001 for watershed protection. Later the Florida Trail was routed through it, and was I ever glad. This place made my top dozen must-see places in the Sunshine State.

That night I sat before the fire, mesmerized by the flames. Saw palmettos on the perimeter reflected the flickering light. I laughed to myself about the anti-fire backpackers who deride fires as the "backpacker's TV" because we just stare into the flames. But I believe this staring to be ingrained in our DNA. Besides, what else were you going to look at during the pitch dark of night?

Fog rolled in again during the night, long after my early retirement in preparation for an early start. In the morning fog I used my headlamp to navigate the old rice plantation dike while returning to the Florida Trail. The path led across boardwalks and through places that needed boardwalks. These woods were barely above the water table and would surely be underwater after a summer storm or two. Full light revealed deer tracks galore. Apparently the hoofed creatures used this path more than hikers did.

After crossing State Road 100, the FT briefly picked up the Palatka–Lake Butler State Trail, slated to be a major addition to parts of the FT later on, eliminating a road walk I was soon to encounter. I spanned Rice Creek on a railroad trestle, then turned north, back onto Plum Creek Timber Property. Trucks were lined up in the fog, and logging noise echoed in the unseen distance. But who was I to lambaste them for cutting trees? I write books for a living. Books are made of paper, and paper is made from trees. For all I know, the paper on which you read these words may have come from trees cut on Plum Creek Timber property.

This parcel of Plum Creek was leased to a hunt club and not open to the general public, therefore the whole area was as attractive as yesterday's tract had been ugly. The cool morn made for easy travel, and four miles later I came upon a wide sandy road. Was this Old Starke Road? If so, Bud's Grocery was a mile distant. I would resupply. The area seemed too remote for an outpost, but east I went, and through the fog Bud's appeared, just east of Old Starke Road, so old that it had never been paved before becoming obsolete. Some retired men were sitting in front of the country store, as they do outside little stores all over the country. I smiled and said hello as I set down my pack. No theft worries here. The folks inside the store made me feel welcome despite my nine-days-since-a-real-shower appearance. I bought a few days' worth of grub and then backtracked to catch the FT as it headed west. I hated backtracking or getting off the trail, but this was a planned stop and the larder was getting a little low. To keep the backpack light, my strategy was to carry little and restock as often as practicable, even at the higher prices the local stores offered as opposed to better full-service grocery stores.

The fog had broken into a warm and sunny day by the time I reached Caraway Mail Route Road. I traced the road north, passing one lone house before entering Etoniah Creek watershed, shared by Etoniah Creek State Forest and Etoniah Creek Hunt Club. The former mail route, now devoid of all mail, had devolved into a rutted, sandy track bordered by pine trees. Open to the sun overhead and not showing signs of recent rains, the white road sand was loose and made for slow, exertion-filled walking. Who says hiking in Florida is easy? If you aren't in a swamp, you get sand; or if not sand, then sand hills; or sun-baked flat lands of clumped grass, or limestone solution holes covered in water, or faint trails through bald cypress. The challenges of the Florida Trail are soon apparent to those who hike it.

A long downhill led to a sharp turn and a bridge over dark Etoniah Creek, and the now shady trail turned upstream and entered the Etoniah Creek Gorge. While the term *gorge* was a little ambitious, the stream did cut a valley upward of fifty feet deep, gorge-ous by Florida standards. Etoniah Creek snaked through a forest made lush by the shade-giving hills that surrounded it. Narrow footbridges spanned clear creeklets that flowed off the hills down to Etoniah.

Once again the Florida Trail did it—ambling along then hitting a particular stretch where the scenery became spectacular. The beauty seemed to be where the water was, the wetter the better. But wetter always meant more difficult to build a trail. That was why, even here, much of the trail threaded along the edge of the ravine. It offered vistas down into the creek, including one particularly pretty

The Iron Bridge shelter was deluxe.

area where a spur trail went to the rim of the gorge, overlooking the confluence of blackish Etoniah Creek and the shallower, tan-colored Falling Branch.

The Florida Trail then began tracing Falling Branch beyond the confluence and I reached my destination, Iron Bridge shelter. This trail shelter was deluxe, with a front porch leading to a fully enclosed and screened wooden sleeping area. I called it the Iron Bridge Inn. A watery cleanup preceded digging into a few goodies from Bud's Grocery, which I munched, basking in the nearly perfect weather. I couldn't help but wonder how cold it might be back home in Johnson City, or what other weather surprises were in store, ahead on the Florida Trail.

12

The Long Green Tunnel

The Iron Bridge shelter was as envisioned; it was the bridge itself that was perplexing. From the name I had conjured up an image of a structure robust and big enough for a car. The bridge, however, was but a single iron "plank" dropped across Falling Branch, which flowed out of Georges Lake. While contemplating bridges, my eyes followed the darting movements of all the shelter's lizards. They liked the Iron Bridge Inn, too. The little critters would cling motionless to the side of the structure, or masquerade on the porch, or repose in the leaf litter on the ground, then skitter manically to another spot, to remain motionless again. They liked it hot—the hotter the better—and thus were happy this warming afternoon.

I was officially in North Florida, according to the *Florida Trail Companion Guide*, and nearing the halfway point, which the book proclaimed to be near Keystone Heights. An exact, definable halfway point did not exist, because halfway depended on the decisions you made back at the two major decision points down south.

Drip, drip, drip. Drip, drip, drip on the tin roof of the Iron Bridge shelter. I awoke to rain. I stumbled to the porch to check out the unexpected precipitation. The drips were primarily among the trees and not in the clearing in front of the shelter. Ah, not rain, but fog so dense that it was condensing on the trees and dripping down onto the shelter roof. It was 5:00 a.m., so I stayed awake and broke camp. "Onward through the fog" became my hiking motto as I greeted dawn again on foot, heading west, now in the Etoniah Creek State Forest in low, wet oak woods. The path wound above the Falling Branch bottoms, where I startled four-legged creatures darting away into the veil of moisture: deer. Ahead the trail made a parking area, where a sign recommended a reroute around a timber operation in the state forest. Keeping with the blazes, I presumed to be on the reroute, but alas, I was not, and miles later I finally hit the timbered area. It's hard to follow tree blazes when the trees are gone, but I managed to trace the old footbed through the leftover brush and pockets of trees still standing. When I lost the footbed of the trail, I angled northwest, popping out in sight of where the Florida Trail left the state forest. Sometimes having twenty-plus years of backpacking behind you pays off. Other times it makes you think you can try things or go places you shouldn't. But I'll never stop trying.

A road walk connected the state forest to Gold Head Branch State Park, which put me back on foot trail again, rolling through hills and ambling past Little Lake Jackson, where a stone-landscaped hillside picnic area overlooked the lake. I was looking for a park employee, so that I could register for the primitive campsite. The park's auto-accessible campground was near the trailhead and I found a bathhouse to take a shower. The hot water and shave were invigorating. Clean, I returned to the picnic area and spotted a truck occupied by a couple in their late seventies. The park volunteers from Iowa drove me to the office, where I registered and paid a small camping fee, and then gratefully accepted a ride back. It had already been a fourteen-mile day. The sky had fully cleared and was heating up fast.

The half mile from the picnic area to the backcountry campsite concluded another day on the Florida Trail. The campsite had a picnic shelter and overlooked Little Lake Johnson. A hot wind blew from the sand-rimmed lake, delivering little relief from the 80-plus-degree temperature. Rollercoaster up. I was beginning to grasp that the average temperatures given in my literature for Florida locations were just that—averages—whereas I was walking through alternating heat and cold, scarcely encountering temperatures that were ju-u-st right. All the same, better hot than cold, if I were forced to choose.

I returned to Gold Head Branch to get water. The swift, clear, sand-bottomed stream had cut a surprisingly deep ravine. The uppermost parts of these ravines, where branches emerged from the hills, were called steepheads, hence the park's name. The park was one of Florida's first. You can still see the stone structures built by the Civilian Conservation Corps in the 1930s.

This oak-shaded campsite had good camp furniture. I could appreciate that. The camp furniture—a picnic table—was provided by the park. I generally prefer a more rustic atmosphere, with no man-made contraptions, where nature provides the camp furniture of logs against which to lean, or piles of stones (rare in Florida) for seats, or sometimes a rock-wood combination, such as a log placed across a base of stones for an elevated seat. Natural camp furniture was usually a key factor in choosing a campsite. Still, I admit that a picnic table was the most comfortable for sitting, preparing food, and writing.

I hadn't even had the first cup of morning coffee before a sudden shower cut through the lukewarm dawn, each big drop rimmed in a poof of dust as it reached the campsite floor. The shower hastened my camp breaking. I slugged the cup of java and then downed some Cream of Wheat—an alternative mushy breakfast to gagmeal—as if I was in an eating contest at the local county fair.

I trucked along Gold Head Branch, going faster than normal, stomach dancing from the speed-eating, as if I could outrun the rain or deny its inevitability. The morning was perhaps the warmest and certainly most humid yet. I was soon out of the state park and into Camp Blanding, a military installation, where a particularly scenic section of trail passed. Here big hills divided clear lakes, and shaggy live oaks bordered clearer streams. The rain hit again and, judging by the sky, looked as if it had come to stay. I put on the poncho but found it simply stifling, so I used the poncho to cover the backpack. The forest was especially thick along Lake Lowery. Not a soul was to be seen on the National Guard training base. The trail passed Magnolia Lake, where a light breeze pushed drizzle and waves toward me. In its constant search for public land, the FT entered Keystone Heights airport property, where no plane was to be heard. It appeared that everyone except me had received evacuation orders.

I popped out on State Road 100, looking at a substantial road walk from Keystone Heights to the town of Lake Butler. This part of the Florida Trail was to be rerouted onto the Palatka–Lake Butler State Trail. The forty-seven-mile state trail followed the old Norfolk Southern railroad right-of-way between the towns of Palatka and Lake Butler and was slated for extensions in both directions, ultimately connecting St. Augustine to Lake City, a distance of a hundred miles. I had just turned west on County Road 18 under dark, drizzly skies when I passed a freshly run-over deer that looked as if it had eaten a lit stick of dynamite for breakfast. That was enough to send me searching for the Palatka–Lake Butler State Trail, which the map indicated ran parallel to CR 18. I scrambled through the brush and found the trail. Trees had been recently cut and cleared from the old railroad grade. The trail was still under development and not officially open, but I was going to walk it unofficially as far as it would take me.

The rail trail was much more to my taste. When it officially becomes part of the Florida Trail, it will be a major enhancement. Seemingly to keep my newfound enthusiasm in check, the mist turned to rain. I donned the poncho, though still wondering about its value in these ultrahumid conditions of off and on rain. Back off came the plastic protection, and now I was soaked with a combination of sweat and rain. It was not an especially appealing proposition, but then again I was so happy to be on the rail trail that I didn't give a darn, even when it crossed creeks on dubious trestles undoubtedly to be replaced. The trail aimed northwest, where an increasingly dark sky turned ominous. A big storm and I were on a crash course.

I looked for a campsite but was in a swampy area, so I hurried on until I found a spot in some planted pines with needles several inches deep. I took the poncho off the pack, tied some string to its corners, and connected the string to the pines. I staked one side of the poncho to the ground, the side facing the oncoming storm. The pack stood upright at the other end of the poncho from my head to block wind-driven rain. The poncho became a shelter; a small one, but a shelter. To make this work, you had to have flat, dry ground, just the right trees around, and enough rope, on which I was running low. But it all worked out and I spent the afternoon under the tarp, alternating between lying prone and sitting up, twisting to one side and turning on the other, looking at maps and rereading the *Companion Guide*, planning, plotting, visualizing, and scheming.

A break in the rain allowed me to make a fire with much effort, so as to cook dinner and make coffee. It was also something to do. The shelter was too iffy and the rain too likely to return for me to break out the book writing equipment. I hadn't finished the coffee before the rain resumed, lasting well past dark. There is no upside to camping in the rain, unless you are trapped in a forest fire. It was a long night under the tarp, simply due to the accumulated hours beneath it. In my hovel, I flipped and flopped more than an extra large order of pancakes at the IHOP.

Overnight, the warmth gave way to a cool clear morn, and I continued northwest, tracing the rail trail, which was beelining for Lake Butler and the unknown. Sometimes I had a plan for where to camp, sometimes not. Today's campsite and what I would do were unknown, despite my map perusings. The Palatka–Lake Butler trail was itself the wild card, being not yet formally in service. Would the trail dead-end at a defunct trestle, or would it simply become so overgrown as to be impassable? Would it be gated? However, part of an adventure is knowing that unknowns lie ahead. Where would I camp? What would happen at Lake Butler? Having a day of unknowns could be discomforting to those who prefer the known, who prefer routine and security. What if someone handed you an envelope with the rest of your life detailed inside? Would you open it? Or would you let each day unfold? The fact that the agenda for a day is unknown doesn't mean it will be bad. If it comes to that, every day for everyone is unknown, even if you are in a routine. I expected good outcomes on every unknown day.

I mentally referred to the rail trail as the Long Green Tunnel (I often had conversations with myself, of course, there being no one else with whom I could converse). The trail was bordered by evergreens mostly, and covered with grass. Since it went in a straight line, the greens of the trees and the old railroad bed all merged into a long green tunnel. Deer liked the trail, too; I ran into two small groups of them near the New River. On the map the New River looked like a major waterway. After crossing a series of smaller trestles, I was betting the New River bridge would be defunct, forcing a miles-long backtrack. I decided to leave the Palatka–Lake Butler trail where County Road 235 crossed the old railroad grade. I then cut back over to State Road 100, spanning the New River on the road bridge, and took the road on into Lake Butler. Later I heard that the New River railroad bridge had burned down, so it was a good call.

Lake Butler is the county seat of Union County, the smallest county in the state. The Florida Trail travels directly through this pleasant place. I passed small businesses, houses, and the attractive brick courthouse, restored to become one of the state's most camera worthy. I walked to the west side of town and a laundromat. My first move was to clean my clothes, then I would resupply and see what else was going on here. I threw my first batch of clothes into the washer. A woman, also washing, was unable to hold back her curiosity. She inquired as to my doings, and I mentioned the Florida Trail and how the Palatka–Lake Butler State Trail had saved a long road walk. It turned out that her husband had been on the crew that removed the old railroad tracks—"Oooh, twelve or thirteen years ago."

Cleanly dressed, I moved on to visit the grocery store, library, and an outdoor store, toting my pack with me as if it were a sack of gold I couldn't leave unattended. After all, it was my everything—for the time being. I scored more rope to hang the tarp better, as further rains were expected, despite the beautiful day. Resupplied, I took the rail trail southeast, back toward the New River, to camp for the night on the edge of town before proceeding on the next day. The rail trail was well groomed through Lake Butler. Near the last few houses, the trail reached a creek and a washed-out trestle, with a few creosote-soaked timbers still forming a monument to what had once been. I managed to descend into the steep ravine and cross the creek using an old railroad tie laid across the dark water. After scrambling back up to the railroad grade I headed on, thinking how agonizingly slowly the Palatka–Lake Butler trail was being developed. It was a jewel in the rough and will be a fine addition to the Florida Trail.

The Union County Courthouse is one of the state's most camera worthy.

The edges of town are great places to camp. You can get heavy, fresh foods and not have to carry them far. I enjoyed a heavy meal that night. Think of something heavy that you would like to eat but wouldn't want to carry far—a watermelon, for example. Later I got up to hunt for some wood and noticed a light through the trees. Perhaps I'd camped a little too close to the edge of town. However, no one came; no one noticed the smoke. I guessed no one was outside, as a chill had ridden in on the increasing wind. I went to add a layer of clothing to beat the chill, my long-sleeved T-shirt, and couldn't find it. Oops—it had been the last item in the dryer, its neckline still a little damp. Then I'd just walked away. How could someone with a grand total of three shirts leave one of them behind, I ask you?

The first order of morning business would be to buy another shirt or retrieve my own, though I doubted it was sitting in that dryer. I walked into town to the Dollar General, but it was still closed, so I walked back to the laundry to find the lost shirt. There I was, backtracking, rewalking through a *town*, waiting for the opening of a store I didn't want to patronize, in order to replace a shirt I had stupidly lost. Self-created predicament. And rain was predicted, followed by a cold spell. Before starting out on the long hike, I had known irritating moments like this would come. It happens, and all one can do is persevere. The time had come. The moment was here.

Strangely enough, Lake Butler stood dead quiet on this overcast Saturday morning, like a prop town waiting for the actors to come onto the set. I felt as though I was waiting for a director to come out and tell me where to go and what to say. Just before I reached the laundromat, a live human, a man in glasses, crossed the street, striding directly for me. From ten feet away he asked—you've guessed it— "Are you hiking the Florida Trail?" He asked my name. I told him. He was Frank Orser, and he was with two other Florida Trail Association members, Brad and Elizabeth, in Lake Butler to maintain the section of trail in the Lake Butler Forest, just north of town. I explained my shirt problem, and he offered to take me to the Laundromat, which was in sight. Of course the shirt wasn't there. If the new owners of that shirt had known how dirty it had been while in my possession, would they have kept it? Sensing my displeasure with the situation, Frank insisted that I literally take the shirt off his back, a long-sleeved T-shirt; he had on another underneath. What a guy! Just when things got to this stupidly low ebb, the situation turned around on a dime.

I thanked Frank and visited with the trail crew before they went on to Lake Butler Forest, while I resupplied at the IGA grocery store, this time with lighter stuff to be carried long distance. The grocery was quiet. A checkout girl, not twenty years old, thin, with brown hair and glasses, let me put my backpack near her while I shopped. When I paid for my groceries she asked me, "What do you expect to see on the Florida Trail?" This time I replied, "Nature." She said from behind her lenses, "Well, there's nothing but woods and swamps here, so you came to the right place." I submitted that woods and swamps were better than the traffic and crime of some big city, but she persisted in her longing to leave Lake Butler.

As I left the IGA, walked outside, and began to load the goods in my pack, a woman dressed in yellow stopped. She had been in line behind me and said, "She needs to leave here before she can come back and appreciate it." Amen, sister. Sometimes we can't accurately value family, friends, and experiences in the places where we were raised until we no longer have them. The clichés have it. Sometimes we have to get out and check whether the grass is really greener on

Frank Orser gave his time to the Florida Trail and his clothes to a forgetful hiker.

the other side of the fence before we can figure out that there's no place like home.

Loaded, I moved on and was soon in Lake Butler Forest. Brad and Elizabeth were repainting blazes. Frank was ahead clearing brush, his orange Florida Trail Association ball cap hanging low over his glasses. Despite being of retirement age, Frank was clearly in shape. His gloved hands could swing an adze, a brush-clearing tool, with the best of 'em. The shirt he still wore and the shirt he had given me presented other clues. Both were T-shirts from running events. Frank was a runner and probably more. I thanked him again for the shirt and later regretted not learning more about him, though I did learn he was a giving man, giving his time to the Florida Trail and his clothes to a forgetful hiker.

Lake Butler Forest was also owned by Plum Creek Timber, this parcel let as hunt leases. The FT here was advertised as extremely wet and it did not disappoint, traveling through a variety of environments but wet in nearly all of them, including row-cropped pines, creeks, and swamps of maple, sweetgum, tupelo, and cypress. I had mentioned my "the wetter the better" theory of beauty on the Florida Trail to Frank, and he had said, "Then you'll like this section." And it was pretty, but a little more wet than scenic. The forest was dead quiet and still. My sporadic sloshing was the only sound. I kept expecting the first rain drops from the murky sky, but they still had not fallen before I reached the Swift Creek campsite. A laurel oak centered the grassy clearing overlooking Swift Creek, which really was swift. Someone had attached a miniature American flag to the oak. A good sign.

It was fine to be back in the woods, solitude notwithstanding. Solitude never bothered me too much, though. As a hiker and writer, I often take work trips alone for weeks or months at a time, hiking trails, paddling rivers, exploring campgrounds, and doing the write-ups. Friends may join me now and then as they did on this trip, but it is often hard for people to get away for long. Besides, I was working, and writing is solitary anyway. You and I are not going to sit side by side at a computer and each type with one hand. So solitude was par for the course. The times when I wished for company were while experiencing superlative beauty in nature and wishing others could share the moment.

Heavy rains were predicted, so I set up the poncho/tarp and waited for the storms. And waited, and waited. I began to feel like a slave to the weather radio, reacting to its declarations as surely as a servant to a master. Sometimes, when you know it is going to rain, you just want it to get here already, then go on its wet way. The rain came only after midnight, lightning and thunder included. I hunkered a little deeper in the bag, after breaking out the light to make sure all was well and dry. The little poncho/tarp made most moist situations a close call. And when it was raining hardest, mist drifted in. But if I had wanted to stay perfectly dry I would have lugged a tent. Using the poncho/tarp was simply a bet. I was betting that the five-ounce shelter would keep me dry enough to make it through with a mere modicum of discomfort and would keep my stuff dry most of the time, and indeed

Heavy rains were predicted, so I set up the poncho/tarp and waited for the storm.

it did. What it did not do was keep mosquitoes at bay. This time I wanted a sure-fire rain-proof setup over bug proofing. Adding the bug netting under the tarp complicated the structure, so during the night I lathered on a little bug dope where my skin was showing.

Day came, and I was a few bites the worse for wear, but dry. I left camp under a slowly clearing sky on a trail made even wetter by the night's rains. Lake Butler Forest exceeded its wet reputation, with miles of watery walking. The highlight was crossing a deep cypress stand, South Prong Swamp. This was the upper reach of the South Prong St. Marys River. The main St. Marys River forms the easternmost boundary between Georgia and Florida. Both the main St. Marys and Florida's hallmark river, the Suwannee, start in Georgia's Okefenokee Swamp. The Suwannee lay ahead. I really was getting to the top of Florida, both elevationally and in map view. The north wind grew brisker and cooler as the day came on. Eight miles later I made the second campsite in Lake Butler Forest, located near a pond amid some slash pines with enough low-lying brush and other trees to block the north wind.

At camp I pondered family and friends and strangers. Nobody knew where I was; I didn't know where anyone else was either. I hadn't seen another person all day long.

The afternoon was my day in the sun. Enjoying the heat from above, I watched the pines sway in the wind. Maine is called the Pine Tree State, but the name would fit just as well for Florida, which has pines from the Keys to the mouth of the St. Johns River in the north and to the Perdido River in the west. Pines are really amazing trees, especially if you take time to study them while lying on your back. With no distractions. Crumbly dry bark surrounds a fibrous center, which rises forth from the ground looking much too thin to support the superstructure of branches extending outward to their ends, where even thinner green needles absorb enough energy from the sun to keep the tree going. As they grow, the lower limbs atrophy, losing their usefulness, and upward the trunk and branches grow until the crown reaches an apex where a few needles continue ever upward toward the sky. On a windy day like this one, the tallest trees, exposed to the most blow, would sway back and forth more than ten feet in any direction. As the trees swayed, the needles swayed too, independent of the tree. Let me assure you it all plays better under brilliantly blue skies broken by contrasting white clouds, lit by an almost spring sun growing stronger all the time. The land sets the stage but weather sets the tone.

Overnight, the weather rollercoaster dove into frostland, but I stayed pretty warm by the fire, stoking it through the hours of darkness. Having a fire already going in the morning makes it a lot easier to arise, even when it is 5:00 a.m. I was back on the FT at daylight and hadn't gone a hundred yards before the first foot dunking. By now I need hardly note that walking through water is to be expected in Florida and isn't necessarily unpleasant. However, walking through water at 35 degrees is unpleasant. The first wet steps were chilling. I had to make up my mind to minimize the unpleasantness by proceeding on until the air warmed and I could find a sunny spot in which to expose my toes to the sun. This morning hike was like going to the dentist—it had to be done, even if you didn't like it. I knew that when looking back on the adventure, moments like this would recede into the background. Besides, would I rather be walking through a swamp than sitting in the traffic jam going on all over the East Coast about this time? No question.

The unevenness of terrain made this swamp slog troublesome, walking over linear undulations. When pines are row-cropped in wet areas, the soil is built up along the rows of pines, leaving little ditches between the rows. Over time, the ditches round off, but going across rows necessitated the up and downs over the moguls. My numb stumps weren't as up to this task as to standard trail walking.

The sun began hitting the treetops. A warm-up was inevitable. I reached US Highway 90, left the Lake Butler Forest behind, and entered the Osceola National Forest at Olustee Battlefield, the site of Florida's biggest Civil War engagement. In early 1864, Union forces at the then small town of Jacksonville headed westward in North Florida to cut off Confederate supply lines of food coming from the state, and to disrupt the turpentine, cotton, and timber industries. They were also to rustle up some Union loyalists in case they could capture Tallahassee, the state capital. Olustee was the only dry east-west passage, which is why US 90 and a railroad run through here today.

The Confederate generals knew that Ocean Pond blocked passage to the north, and a vast swamp (through which I had just walked) lay to the south. The narrow land passage of Olustee was the logical place to stop the passage of matériel and thousands of men. On February 7, 1864, the Union and the Rebels clashed among the tall pines. The grassy understory provided little cover for defense. The battled lasted until dusk, smoke rising from the guns as men tried to fire from behind the pines, and fired upon one another in the open. The Union retreated at dark, and the Confederates continued to preserve Tallahassee as the only Rebel capital not taken in the War of Northern Aggression. The price was high, with over 2,400 casualties among the combatants. This was proportionally one of the bloodiest battles of the entire Civil War. Today the battlefield is a state park, a memorial to slain Confederate soldiers standing tall over the park.

I walked through the field and looked at the memorials. With the sun streaming upon them through the trees, I imagined the battle, and the blood spilled, and the chaos, and the utter dissimilarity of it all from the serene morning I saw, when birdsong rang through the pines.

I passed Cobb Camp and turned toward where the sun was to set. I called this spot the Great Western Turn. For the Florida Trail, this is the point where it begins aiming for the far side of the Panhandle and marks a point of passage for any thru-hiker. The trail had angled west before, but now it was firmly heading westward for the duration of the hike. If it went much farther north it would wind up in Georgia.

Conditions did not change much in the Osceola National Forest. It was wet too, but not as wet as the row-cropped Lake Butler private forest. Just as temperatures vary year to year, so does rainfall. This was a wet year to be on the FT up here. The upside was more water to drink; the downside, more water to slog through. I sloshed about five miles and intersected the entrance road to Ocean Pond Campground. The sun was high now, and I ambled down the paved car path to reach the waterfront camping area, finding a campsite complete with stacked wood left by the previous campers. The car camping site, with picnic table, lantern post, and metal fire ring, wasn't backcountry, but Ocean Pond—neither ocean nor pond—is one of Florida's prettiest bodies of water. The oval lake is a mile or more across, bordered by a low line of trees. Trees also ringed the shoreline next to my camp. I kicked back, barefoot in the sun, resting on my laurels at the Great Western Turn.

The colors were vibrant over Ocean Pond at sunset, cypress trees draped in Spanish moss silhouetted against a kaleidoscopic sky mutating from orange to red to pink, all reflecting off the now stilled water. The sky faded to black and brought a chill, but the stacked wood kept me warm.

13

Strawberry-Blonde or Red?

I was expecting company on the new day. Tina Dean was meeting me at Ocean Pond, and we were to travel the Florida Trail together for the next eleven days. At 2:00 p.m., the appointed rendezvous time, I waited at the trailhead where the FT crossed the entrance road to Ocean Pond Campground. And I waited and waited. I prefer to be prompt, and the price of my efficiency and timeliness was to play the waiting game. However, for someone to be late, someone else had to be waiting for that late someone. My lot in life was to be the waiter. While waiting I did get to see a splendid aerial show. An osprey was challenging a bald eagle for reasons known only to them. The osprey dive-bombed and incessantly squawked and otherwise hassled our national bird and drove it out of my view. Osprey 1, Eagle 0.

Tina showed up at 5:00, driven to the trailhead by a shuttle operator out of White Springs. I was happy to see her and to end the waiting game. An Ohio transplant from a small town near Dayton, she had gone to Kent State University before deciding to follow her parents down to the hills of East Tennessee, where they had moved after her high school graduation. She then transferred to the University of Tennessee and decided to stay. We had met at Trail Days in Damascus, Virginia, an event celebrating the Appalachian Trail. I'd been peddling books and she was enjoying the festivities. What impressed me about her was the determination she showed to attend the event. Prior to Trail Days she had twisted her ankle severely, so she had rented a wheelchair for the weekend in order to follow through with her plan to check out Trail Days. Persistence and ingenuity in one fell swoop.

We loaded my pack with the supplies she had brought and hurried off to beat the sunset, needing to make a little more than three miles to a trail shelter. We caught up while rapidly splashing through numerous wet areas. She had just been on an overnight paddling trip with her brother Nick down the Ocklawaha River, where they had come upon a couple who had capsized in their two-man kayak. The woman was hysterical, the man helpless; Tina had assisted them to shore and back into their boat. What is a woman to do when she comes upon boaters pinned against a tree, screaming and crying? Her delay was completely warranted.

We crossed Interstate 10, where drivers were going places at thirty times our pace. The trail shelter was not far off, located along moving water in an area of large pines. We settled in. Tina finally got to relax, take off her straw hat, and fully display her pigtails, after her day of saving lives, organizing shuttles, and switching from boat camping to backpacking. She surprised me with steaks and even a Diet Coke, my favorite beverage.

The drone of I-10 was audible and continued through dawn. People were going places all night long. We stopped hearing them when we resumed hiking through pine-palmetto woods wet from the rain of late: we were sloshing. Some of the hiking was through row-cropped pines, some where the trees aligned themselves naturally. The works of man are most often done using angles. Look at buildings, roads, furniture. The works of nature flow using curves and seemingly random placement. The pines distinctly demonstrated the differences between the works of man and nature. We picked up an old railroad grade as it headed due north on a straight line, demonstrating again the precision of man's works as it knifed through the hodge-podge trees. The forest had regrown from a long-ago cutting, and the tram road was the only evidence that logging had ever taken place here. We underestimate the recuperative powers of nature. The old tram passed through a recent burn. The lack of ground cover after the fire revealed the grade more clearly. Old ties were still visible. Boardwalks had replaced old bridges that once held locomotives pulling flatbed log-laden railcars.

The FT abruptly left the grade and headed due west, passing through flooded woods, then gained just enough elevation in an oak pine forest to allow us a dry campsite. This first day of March had warmed to the upper seventies, so we found a shady spot, satisfied with our ten-mile day. The upside of the flooded woods was that we could easily collect water. Otherwise this camp would have been waterless.

The standing water combined with the heat had brought out the mosquitoes and Tina swatted away the afternoon, unaccustomed to the swamp angels as yet. I secretly laughed behind a book as the little naggers hovered around her. Let somebody else get bitten for a while. Seemingly for her benefit, the weather was nearly ideal that night, with just enough chill to send the skeeters packing and warrant a campfire. Tina's long strawberry-blonde, sometimes red locks reflected the firelight as she repeatedly remarked on the warm weather. She had endured most of an East Tennessee winter. Ironically, despite much of the forest being flooded, the parts that were dry were bone dry, so we were judicious with our campfire, keeping it small and clearing any flammable brush well away from the burning zone.

The next day, a ten-mile road walk brought us to the banks of the Suwannee River. During the walk I watched blue-eyed Tina and thought about her backpacking history. Living in the shadow of the Smokies had built up in her a hankering to hike and spend the night in yon mountains. She recruited her dad, and the two of them went to a place called Gregory Bald, toting scrounged-up gear typical of first timers. Naturally they got a late start, finishing the climb in the dark, and illegally slept on top of the grassy mountaintop after setting up a camp of sorts using their misappropriations. The star show that night and the next day's highland scenery had her hooked. Subsequently, Tina began buying her own stuff—a backpack, a camp stove, and a sleeping bag I called Stinky. The down bag smelled strange, but Tina thought it smelled good; I believe she associated the malodorous bag with good times she'd had while backpacking. By now she had added some trekking poles, which are used like ski poles for balance and leverage while hiking. The poles gave the thirty-year-old woman an air of walking with purpose.

The Florida Trail made a gorgeous track along the bluffs above the Suwannee River. Below, a white froth moved fast, created from the upstream drop at Big Shoals, one of Florida's natural wonders and easily the Sunshine State's biggest rapids. The FT had once traveled by Big Shoals, but a private property issue had forced a reroute, adding road walk mileage. Sometimes the trail has suffered setbacks. The FT needs to go by Big Shoals. Perhaps the problem will eventually be resolved, and someday it will once again pass alongside the impressive rapids.

On the Suwannee below Big Shoals, the FT made an undulating track along wooded banks where tree duff overlay white sand, deposited during times of flood. Overhead, live oaks mingled with sweetgum, scrub oaks, pine, and holly, forming a green hiking passageway. Thickets of saw palmetto bordered the track. Tupelo and cypress created wooded ramparts along the river. We had extensive views of the Suwannee, which I began to see as a forthcoming cool respite from the long hot day. This was the longest stretch where the Florida Trail followed a major river. We would be under its influence for more than a week.

Ahead, the trail dipped to a feeder stream, just as black as the river itself. A log allowed us to cross dry shod. We climbed away from the feeder stream, reaching a sandy promontory jutting out between the creek and the river. The level locale had a picnic table bearing the Florida Trail logo. Here, we decided, was our camp. The logo had sealed the decision. The river had an early March chill to it, but that didn't stop us from washing off and cooling down in its fast, deep waters. The heat of the afternoon sun was less threatening now, with shade from a nearby oak and with a river that promised to cool us down more than we needed. Tina had brought a tent, so we set it up. The tributary just behind the tent gurgled through the mild foggy night, becoming audible as the evening wind died. This was a Florida Trail first, camping along a singing stream. A gurgling waterway makes a great sleep enhancer.

Numerous pines had the long "cat faces" and metal plate draining devices from when they were bled for sap, which was turned into turpentine.

I couldn't shake the get-up-at-five routine and arose in the dark; Tina slept in until six. We were off and hiking by seven, climbing a steep bluff just beyond a place known as Waldron's Landing. This was the FT's steepest grade yet. The path leveled atop a bluff, overlooking the swift but silent Suwannee.

More often the FT was on a berm of land just above the river bank, with the river on one side and an overflow swamp on the other. The path itself cut through dense saw palmetto thickets. At times, the trail would dip to small tributaries cutting miniature sand valleys as they flowed into the Suwannee. Most of these branches drained the overflow swamps. Tina and I separated at the US Highway 41 bridge over the river. I went on along the Florida Trail, following the river for five miles to make the west side of White Springs, whereas Tina took US 41, entering the small river town from the east to ready her kayak for the trip down the Suwannee. The plan from this point was for her to paddle the river in her kayak, while I hiked the FT, which roughly paralleled the river. We would rendezvous in the afternoon at a camp suitably close to the trail and the river. I liked this plan because it allowed her to boat the bulk of the supplies, while I had a light pack with camping gear and little food. She loved the plan because she loves to kayak.

Spring greens were popping out on the river, wildflowers and more, though most of the trees were still just budding out. While walking solo I came upon the remnants of an old turpentining operation. Numerous pines in the area had the long "cat faces" and metal plate draining devices still in them, from when they had been bled for sap, which was turned into turpentine. I crossed the Suwannee on a road bridge, intersecting the route I had taken in a previous Florida traveling adventure. On that trip, I had left the Okefenokee Swamp in Georgia and paddled a canoe down the Suwannee River, under this very bridge and on downstream to the Gulf of Mexico and the town of Suwannee. From the port, I paddled a sea kayak south along the Gulf all the way to the Keys. This journey of more than two months I describe in *From the Swamp to the Keys: A Paddle through Florida History*.

White Springs is about as much of a trail town as exists on the Florida Trail. It is certainly an outdoors town. Its proximity to the Suwannee River, the Florida Trail, and several state parks, preserves, and wildlands has resulted in a tourist industry that serves people like Tina and me. The White Springs outfitter she had used to shuttle her to Ocean Pond would pick her up miles down and days later on the Suwannee River.

I passed through town without stopping and entered Stephen Foster State Park, which abuts White Springs. The FT entered the well-groomed grounds, where azaleas bloomed in technicolor. I met Tina at the canoe launch. She was packing supplies into the boat, deciding what to bring, what not to bring, and how to arrange it all. She was turning her yellow kayak into a barge. I hit the trail while she took her car back to the outfitter in town. Now we would see whether our hike and float plan would work.

14

One by Land, One by River, Two at Camp

A bell tolled at the park's tower as I left. It was time to go. Tina would meet me downriver at a campsite I would find.

The Suwannee River got its name from a Spanish mission in the 1700s, San Juan Guacara. The river was called the Little San Juan. Mix in local dialect and misspellings on assorted maps, and stir well over time, and you end up with Suwannee. The alligator got its name in a similar way, when the Spanish word *el lagarto*, the lizard, was corrupted to alligator.

The trail stayed scenic through the state park. Spanish moss swathed the trees, adding that Florida touch. River birches hung over the water. Azaleas bloomed. The State of Florida had done a good job picking a riverside location to laud the Suwannee River and the songwriter who wrote what is now the Florida state song, Stephen Foster's "Old Folks at Home," known from New York to New Delhi as *Way down upon the Swanee River . . .*

Humming the tune on the Florida Trail, I left the state park to cross a series of riverside private lands and then reentered land belonging to the Suwannee River Water Management District (SRWMD), where I found a sandbar for camping seven miles down. The beach campsite was on a bend overlooking an oak-topped bank across swirling black waters. SRWMD lands cover fifteen counties with a mission to protect and manage the region's water supply for the natural water systems and for public use, not only the Suwannee but six other rivers in its basin. SRWMD has acquired 315 miles of river frontage along the Suwannee and other rivers it manages. The Florida Trail made extensive use of these lands on its way to the Panhandle.

I jumped into the river, dried off in the sun, and waited for Tina. She rolled up about five that afternoon, smiling and recounting her paddle. She'd met a fellow kayaker who was paddling the Suwannee to the Gulf. I helped her unburden the overloaded kayak. She had two coolers strapped onto the plastic craft, full of tasty edibles that were a definite upgrade from my hiking fare of late. She whipped out folding camp chairs, a true luxury for this trail dog. In the evening dark we hung out on the sandbar listening to bluegrass music, which Tina likes, discussing whether bluegrass was country music or its own genre. Like me, Tina is a passionate arguer and no fence sitter. Her face turns red, concealing her freckles, when she makes a point strenuously.

Tina donned her camp chef hat at the sandbar in the sunny morning, making pancakes from scratch, to be topped with real maple syrup and blueberries. We won't mention the fact that she used tomato- and garlic-flavored olive oil to grease the frying pan. The pancakes would've been great. After breakfast she hung around camp, taking her time, knowing she could get downstream much faster than I would. I loaded up and continued down the Florida Trail, now much more undulating. It dipped into ravines and climbed up bluffs, led down to creeklets and then inevitably rose to parallel the river again. At Interstate 75, the trail once again intersected civilization's infrastructure, passing under the interstate. I had no gripes, since I use I-75 all the time myself. I also use the energy of transmission lines and talk on land line telephones served by the wires I passed underneath. I use the infrastructure; I accept the infrastructure.

Beyond I-75 the FT left the river's edge, instead wandering away from the Suwannee through overflow swamps, some of which were standing pools. Others had streamlike outflows that I had to cross. It took some deft jumping to avoid wetting my feet. The Suwannee River had recently been flooded and high. When the gauge at White Springs showed sixty-two feet or above, parts of the Florida Trail were flooded and hiking it was not recommended. The river had been as high as sixty-seven feet lately but had now dropped to sixty feet. This was typical of how the Florida Trail experience kept working out well for me.

The area was good habitat for wild turkey and deer, both of which I startled. On higher ground, I came upon more turpentining evidence and more cat-faced trees. Below me, the Suwannee flowed dark under limestone bluffs and beside sandbars that it had created while in a brown flooding tumult. The deepest creeks meeting the Suwannee were bridged. One of them, Jerry Branch, was backed up by the high Suwannee, completely submerging the span. Luckily a high water route, a blue-blazed bypass, led to an easier crossing well away from the river. Delicate ferns unfurled along Jerry Branch, holding their spring banners high.

The Florida Trail began climbing as never before, rising over bluffs 125 or more feet above the river, then precipitously descending to creeks that had deeply incised the bluffs. I crossed No Name Creek on a bridge, then ascended a hill so sheer that a metal cable had been attached to a tree at the bluff top to aid hikers on the climb. I declared this stretch to be the steepest on the entire Florida Trail; I still think it is. The ups and downs continued on a cane-bordered track, taxing unused muscles meant for mountain hiking. The trail left SRWMD land, passing into Crooked Branch Ranch, a failed real estate development later sold lot by lot. Now the FT crossed the ranch lot by lot.

There I met Dan Morgan, a slow-talking, sense-making native Floridian owner of a riverfront house. The trail went between his abode and the river. In his fourteen years there, he'd had nothing but positive experiences with hikers, and he considered the trail going through his backyard an honor and an asset. Dan had no formal agreement with the FTA about the trail passing across his land; he openly wondered if he should have one. Many lots in Crooked Branch Ranch were bought by the SRWMD, and others were being developed or had a half-built house on pilings, forgotten and underfunded projects. In places like these the path of the FT is ever in peril, as the kindness of the landowners allows the trail to pass through their property. All it would take would be one bad experience with one bad trail user and the trail might have to be rerouted, taking it away from the river for miles, as had happened back at Big Shoals.

Dan wished me luck on my thru-hike, and I proceeded on. Devils Mountain marked the apex of the Suwannee Bluffs. Devil's club, a thorny vine that you don't want to touch, grew here. The bluff itself offered southward views through the trees for untold miles, an expansive green vista to the far horizon. Once again, the Florida Trail surprised. This truly was a day of superlatives—the highest bluffs, the longest land view, the biggest climbs, the most continuous ups and downs. The Sunshine State showed off some of its finest scenery along its most famous river.

Ahead, the trail and the river parted ways for some distance. I kept scouting for a spot where they reunited and where Tina could land her kayak. Once I found a suitable place, I tied a bandana to a tree overhanging the Suwannee, marking the spot. She pulled up later that afternoon, having given me a nearly three-hour head start before traveling twelve river miles, while I had walked thirteen trail miles. We walked back and forth through a narrow ravinelike passage between our camp and the river, unloading the boat and setting up camp in the lee of some live oaks, their spreading limbs shading us. It was Saturday, and the weekend warriors were on the warpath, floating down the river in groups, laughing and splashing and playing and generally having a good time, except for one couple who seemed likely to launch divorce proceedings at the end of their float trip.

That night the chill came on again, and the rollercoaster dipped to 34 degrees before dawn, which I greeted with a fine oak fire. Light revealed waves of fog drifting over the river. I left the camp early, getting my head start to find the next camp. Ahead, I clambered over the raised berm of old US Highway 129, now just a winding ribbon of crumbling asphalt with a faded yellow streak running down its center. I thought of the now old people who had driven now old cars along this once new highway crossing the Suwannee River. The river flowed then and flows now, carving its valley, seeking its level, flowing to the Gulf of Mexico day and night, day and night, year after year, easily outlasting federal highways. Despite the chill, the sun was rising, the air was warming, and spring would not be denied. Many trees were budding—maple, musclewood. The first cypresses were raising their spring flags, too. My spirit was lifted by these sightings. The joy of the outdoors is to live and die with the weather and the seasons, reveling in the changes; I was watching with anticipation as time was awakening all that flew, grew, crawled, and swam into spring.

The Florida Trail crossed an abandoned railroad line, which in turn had once crossed the Suwannee. The bridge supports were still intact but their span was gone, a reminder that the greatest of transportation plans can fall by the wayside. The disused road and railroad seemed affirming: I relied on foot power as the FT worked up a long gradual slope rising above the river, offering ideal conditions for magnolia, cedar, and wildflowers aplenty. The calendar still said winter, but the Suwannee said spring. As during the day before, the trail undulated, but the banks were generally lower, moderating the ups and downs. I worked around creeks here, too, but along with the river, they were falling. Sinkholes were more common trailside features now. Rocks. Rocks formed the lips of some sinks. The hint of hills and rocky streams conjured up home. I missed it but stayed true to a motto of mine, "Wherever you are, be there." Enjoy the moment. Don't look too far ahead, thinking about where you are going to be, or spend too much time reflecting on where you've been. We all know people whose glory days were in high school and who continue to wax lyrical about that era, retelling the same stories, adding more detail, building the memories into invincible battleships of good times that can't be sunk or replaced.

The trail wound over land bridges between the numerous sinkholes. Some were shallow bowls, others rocky and vertical. Still others were wooded; some were filled with water. Between these sinkholes and the springs along the Suwannee's banks, I was seeing the signals of one complicated underground plumbing system in that limestone labyrinth beneath the earth's surface. Part of SRWMD's mission was to protect the plumbing by protecting the land above it.

Finding a good campsite was important since, in actuality, we were spending more time at the campsites than on the river or trail. It was at the campsites that we could really soak in the atmosphere, having a still view of the scenery rather than moving through it. At camp we would watch day turn to night. I was looking for camp. Holly trees grew to massive proportions, dropping thousands of prickly leaves to the ground, making those areas less campable. A bridge spanned Mitchell Creek, made slack by the high Suwannee. As I was crossing, a pair of deer splashed across the creek, not choosing to use the span. I had entered Holton Creek Wildlife Management Area, and protected lands on both sides of the river lent a wild atmosphere where the sounds of nature reigned. The Suwannee had more civilized options, however, with the development of the Suwannee River Wilderness Trail—a series of cabins, shelters, and camping areas. I passed through a camping cluster that had a nice boat ramp, screened shelters, and more, but I pushed on, seeking a natural setting sans accoutrements; when it came to campsites, those not showing man's handiwork were supreme.

A sharp bend in the river created a sandbar that would make landing a kayak easy. Several giant live oaks stood inside the bend. They had been overlooking the Suwannee for hundreds of years. I stopped in their shadow and said, "This is it." I waited on their fallen leaf litter after planting the bandana camp flag, which I wore around my neck while hiking. Tina landed on the sandbar, hollering my name, as I was out of sight. She walked the sand, leaving the sunny river for the darker oak woods, and was taken aback by these living giants. That evening a descending sun bathed our oak camp in a yellow glow, making it seem unreal. But it was real, and it was ours for the night.

Tina concocted strawberry pancakes the next morning, using butter instead of flavored olive oil to grease the pan. And they were good. I tore down the Florida Trail with pancake energy, slaloming around sinkholes. The valley was more hole than land surface. Where land was land, expansive clusters of white zephyr lilies created a pale carpet. Royal live oaks lorded it over the woods with their outstretched arms. Pines grew at the highest points. The trail led downhill directly across a body of water. I didn't know where the water came from or went. I did know a ford was necessary, so I took off my shoes

A descending sun bathed our oak camp in a yellow glow.

and socks then barefooted it into the black still water. Rotting leaves squished between my toes, releasing mud clouds into the tannic water. The water rose to mid-thigh, then grew shallow again. After drying off my feet, I proceeded on.

White lilies continued carpeting the trailside terrain by the hundreds as I proceeded along the banks of Holton Creek, which flows into the Suwannee. Zephyr lilies favor moist bottoms. The solitary flower is usually white but sometimes has a pinkish bloom. From here

Where there was land, zephyr lilies created a pale carpet.

forward the river bottoms were snowed over with them, standing out particularly brightly on the overcast morn.

The trail circled around an aquatic upwelling, a black spring, where mysterious and gloomy water emerged from a circular flow to shoot toward the Suwannee. Other springheads emerged nearby. I believe the Holton Springhead to be an outflow of the nearby Alapaha River, though the main upwelling of the Alapaha is at Alapaha Rise, which is downstream on the Suwannee. The Alapaha originates in Georgia, is a major feeder of the Suwannee, and has its own series of quirky flowing patterns. At normal water levels the Alapaha doesn't flow into the Suwannee and offers nothing but a dry riverbed for its last seventeen miles. At high levels the Alapaha fills the riverbed and makes it to the Suwannee in its channel.

I left Holton Spring and continued west on the Florida Trail, which crossed the Alapaha on a road bridge. Indeed, the Alapaha was flowing high. The Florida Trail left the road to trace the Alapaha's banks before rejoining the Suwannee River, which had widened considerably with the addition of the Alapaha. I walked along a high bluff covered in trees, now in Suwannee River State Park. On the outside of a river bend, well above the water, was a campsite. It availed a long sweeping upstream view of the Suwannee. After eating lunch, I leaned against a tree and watched from the bluff for Tina to float this way. Her kayak soon appeared, a yellow speck on the churning molasses, the dark ribbon bordered by green live oaks and red-budded maples. As she came closer, I could distinguish her paddling and gave out a yell. She yelled back and was shortly at the water's edge. We unloaded her gear and hauled it up to the bluff top.

Since it was early, Tina took advantage of the Florida Trail and went for a hike. I was saving my legs, with hundreds of miles yet to walk. That evening a mourning dove cooed. Tina recalled her childhood, listening to the doves from her rural Ohio backyard. Her mom had planted a spruce tree when she was born, and she wondered how the last thirty years had treated it. Mourning doves are found all over North America. These prolific birds migrate annually to avoid winter, just as I do.

The campsite's river sweep faced east, which allowed two coffee drinkers to watch the sun rise over the fog-covered river, mimicking our steaming cups. The slanting rays illuminated the fog and the spring greens and reds, backlighting the dark drapery of Spanish moss hanging still against the light. This spot overlooking the Suwannee River beat any kitchen or diner as a setting for a little morning java. The climbing sun reflected off the water, doubling its intensity and quickly warming the campsite. We soon parted ways, Tina to ply the river, and me to follow my feet, both of us heading down the valley of Florida's river of rivers. It simply couldn't have been a finer March morning. The nip in the air and the warmth of the sun formed an atmospheric elixir that delighted the skin and offered the clarity to enjoy all that lay before our eyes.

Once again the FT left the Suwannee River to work around one of its tributaries, this time the Withlacoochee River, which was nearly equal in size to the Suwannee. They are sometimes called the Twin Rivers. Our next wild campable lands were in the Twin Rivers State Forest. The trail met a road to span a river, this time the Withlacoochee, then left the road and followed the Withlacoochee's downstream meanders, reaching the ghost town of Ellaville. Ideally located at the confluence of the Twin Rivers, Ellaville was a sawmill and manufacturing complex where hundreds once lived, including a former Reconstruction governor of the state, George Drew. But the local pine ran out, the people left, and by 1942 even the post office had shut down. Drew's extravagant mansion fell into disrepair and was abandoned as well. It finally burned in 1970.

The trail returned to the Suwannee, now a broader, bigger river with lower banks and fewer curves. It moved rapidly yet silently, with swirls and boils welling up from unseen influences. Live oaks still dominated the riverside bottomland amid sinks aplenty, and the gently undulating terrain made the hiking easy. Wild azaleas bloomed white and pink. An eleven-mile day brought me to the Black Tract designated campsite. A cool north wind blew as I sat and waited for Tina, who rolled in with more supplies and a few adventures of her own to relate.

That morning she had been on a mission, as our luxurious supplies were running low. At Suwannee River State Park she had met a park volunteer who offered to take her to resupply. Before she knew it, she was bouncing down the road in a pickup truck to the Falmouth General Store. She recounted the tiny store's atmosphere—packed with people getting hot lunches. I could see her carefully plucking groceries off the shelves, leaning over the hunched backs of workmen shoving in lunch.

When she returned to her kayak, two canoeists paddled up, finishing their trip at Suwannee River State Park. Kurt, from the state of Washington, introduced himself, and they chatted about the outdoors. He had been a backpacker before he lost a leg, and now he enjoyed traveling and camping by water. Kurt insisted that Tina rummage through his food bins to help herself to leftovers. She hesitated and then gratefully accepted a half-full bag of peanut M&Ms, some dried milk (the store had run out), and an unopened jar of peaches. She threw her head back in a laugh and proudly handed me a two-liter Diet Coke to chug and last week's news to read. I noticed that her eyes looked sea-green, not blue; her eyes change, like the color of her hair. As we toasted the waning evening with hot chocolate, I was thinking how odd her color changes were.

The Suwannee was heading south and so was I, though I was leaving the river to connect with another unit of the Twin River State Forest. In the forest I heard a rumble of machinery in the distance and came upon a freshly cut fire line. Apparently a controlled burn or prescribed fire was imminent. Most people who live in Florida have doubtless driven through the smoke of a prescribed fire or commented on the haze that such events bring. Some two million acres per year are burned this way. Conditions have to be favorable before starting a fire. Land managers check the wind direction to keep the smoke from going toward smoke-sensitive areas. They also check the fuel moisture level. Proper moisture levels allow managers to control fires better. Prescribed fires are necessary for the overall health of the forest and safety of the people living nearby. Fires help the ecosystem by keeping fire-dependent areas in their natural state, thus preserving the plants and animals of those ecosystems. Prescribed fires are a preventive to out-of-control wildfires that periodically plague the state. Demonstrating the renewability of timber, freshly planted pine seedlings grew next to the future burn area.

Palms increased in the river bottoms. The easy five-mile day brought me to the Mill Creek campsite before noon. Once again Tina and I rendezvoused and enjoyed a last lazy, river day before we would get back into gear. That afternoon I scoured my pack for excess weight, as Tina would be continuing downriver and the Florida Trail was turning away, leaving me to tote the entirety of my supplies. Tina had brought me a new hiking shirt, so I ceremonially burned the old ragged one emblazoned with "Molloy Electric," my brother

I dangled the gray cotton over the fire and it caught, flames licking upward.

Mike's business. Thanking Mike, I dangled the gray cotton over the fire and it caught, flames licking upward. I held it as long as possible, then dropped it into the coals, where it disintegrated into black fragmented flakes. It had worn well.

15

"You Should Have Brought a Canoe"

My pack was one shirt lighter but a little heavier in food as I stumbled through the early morning dark, anticipating a long day crossing private timberlands. You never know what is going to happen later, so you get started sooner, I thought as I passed the last of the hundreds—likely thousands—of live oaks along the Suwannee River. The trail now turned away from the oaks and the river. That was the end of the Suwannee Valley. Tina was floating on down the river for another day, then camping solo that night before the outfitter in White Springs would pick her up at Dowling Park. She would be seeing plenty of the springs for which the Suwannee is known. I'd be drinking swamp water from ditches; that is, from linear wetlands.

The Florida Trail picked up a westbound sand road, open to the sun overhead. The main task here was picking the right part of the sand on which to walk. Sometimes the best way was in a tire track and sometimes it was along the road edge. Where to walk depended on where the surface was neither too hard nor too soft, where it was just right; where the ground would not beat up my feet nor make them dig deeply into the sand, taking one step forward and a half step back.

The sand road led to a gated timberland that made up some of the most remote land in Florida. The trees took years to reach harvesting size and were mostly left alone. Places like this were leased out to hunt clubs, members of which came here in season. Otherwise, the only human presence was the occasional harvest. Noise ahead broke the silence of the forest and I came upon a harvest in progress. Three log haulers, clad in T-shirts stuffed into stained jeans, were standing around a pickup. I said, "Hi." Not thirty feet away a specialized machine was loudly stripping, cutting, then loading pole pine onto the lumber trucks. The efficiency of the stripping machine was amazing. One by one, and fast, the trucks would fill, and one by one, the drivers would drive them to a nearby mill, probably in Perry.

The drivers, in their thirties and with perhaps enough teeth among the lot to fill one mouth, were quite friendly. They pointed out that my next turn was soon forthcoming on the timber road I was following. Beyond the area being logged, they said I would see other cut areas where pines had already been replanted. People want to help. It is their first inclination. Being hurtful takes malice and thought. The loggers inquired about my journey on the FT, asking the usual questions. They offered resupply information and anything else they could do. I left the loggers and stooped for a drink, getting water from a canal dug for fill to elevate the sand track I walked. While sipping, I realized that pure Florida swamp water was flowing through my body.

A twenty-five-mile day went from cold and still to hot and windy. Trees, trees, and more trees, almost all pine, passed before me, seemingly like an old-time cartoon where the characters stand in front of a background that keeps repeating itself. I was making up mileage to offset some of the short days on the Suwannee. Beyond the Econfina River I found a campsite back in a pine stand, found a stick on which to prop my pack, and propped myself against the pack. I lit a cigar, watching the smoke waft upward, and wished for liquid to wet my parched mouth. I'd been too lazy to fill the water bottle before finding camp. I arose, feeling stiff. In East Tennessee this is known as being "stove up." Water bottle in hand, I sought some liquid solace, imagining myself squeaking like an un-oiled Tin Man. Nearby, a linear wetland offered some Taylor County Tonic, guaranteed to grease your joints and turn your veins brown. Back at camp I didn't move much, except to set up the bug netting, puff the cigar, and read the inside of my eyelids.

The next day brought twelve more miles of deserted sand roads through private timber lands. The Florida Trail was scantily blazed, necessitating a lot of map reading and a little backtracking. Somewhere along the way the trail crossed a railroad track. An orange blaze stood prominently on the crossing sign. Ahead was the loud US Highway 19/27, where Tina and I would meet for the last time. I reached the road and found a really deep ditch, where I took a problematic bath. For starters, the ditch was only thirty feet from the busy road, slightly obscured by minimally greening trees. I covertly stripped, then stepped into the cool water, stirring up bottom muck, which dirtied the water in which I was trying to clean off. I nakedly let the muck settle, still as a statue, then lowered my body in without moving my feet, dipping deep enough to wash off. I clambered out of the water and ran behind the thickest of the trees, to drip dry in the sun. Thus clean, I reclothed and headed out to the roadside, where I propped up my backpack and leaned back against it, the very picture of a vagrant.

The one person who knew I wasn't soon pulled over. She and I went to Perry to enjoy the fruits of civilization in the form of a little celebratory lunch at an Italian place recommended by the laundress who worked where my clothes were being washed. I joked to Tina that my next guidebook should be *Laundromats along the Florida Trail*. Everyone in Perry was bend-over-backwards nice. And I appreciated that. We drove to the Aucilla River to camp that night, enjoying a sendoff meal of steaks and retiring to a foggy warm night. Before the sun could break the fog, Tina was dropping me off at US 19/27 where she had picked me up. We said our goodbyes and she drove north to Tennessee, while I would head west, still in timber lands.

And just like that I was alone, left with the pines and the boars and a heavy pack on this sultry Saturday. Mother Nature evidently ordered a hot day to inform any spring-ignorant plants in North Florida to get on the ball and start greening up. The FT came alongside the Econfina once again, where the hardwoods had already gotten the message. Above the planted pines, delicate hues of red, orange, yellow, and light brown signified the initial stages of leafing out. The colors were the same as in the fall, but instead of going dormant, the trees were coming alive. I bridged the Econfina and kept pressing, feeling the full strength and vigor of my hike so far, enjoying the re-munerations of daily hiking despite the full pack and hot day. Small purple and pink violets lined the moist margins between the sand roads and drainage canals by the hundreds, adding up to thousands, all here seemingly for my personal enjoyment, as nary another hu-man was around.

At some point I switched from the Econfina watershed to the Aucilla watershed, but elevation changes in the Taylor County low-lands were as imperceptible as the drainage patterns of the extensive swamps, an organization so subtle and mazelike that it was impos-sible to tell. The sun bore down into afternoon and at fourteen miles I stopped in a shady pine plantation to make camp. The nearby ditch water was stagnant and the heat thick as I reclined against a pine, covered in sweaty dirt. The site was unsatisfactory and the Aucilla was but four miles distant. I decided to push for the river. An added incentive was a two-liter jug of Diet Coke Tina had stashed along County Road 14, two miles away.

The sun had lowered a bit, providing some trailside shade. At the road I grabbed the soft drink, took a long slug of the brown fizz wa-ter, then powered nonstop to the river. A fluid flowing sound drifted toward me. Rapids! Camping near the rushing river and its sonorous rapture was a treat down here in the flatlands of the Sunshine State. I dropped my pack in a clearing above the Aucilla, walked to the swirl-ing black water and went on in, just below the rapid. The water was fine, reenergizing me after the eighteen-mile day. The campsite was nice, too. Holly trees and oaks bordered the leafy flat above the river, along with a few scattered pines. The watery soundtrack completed the picture. Sol lowered. A slight breeze kept the bugs at a minimum. All was well on the Florida Trail. I felt triumphant.

A full moon was already up by dark, casting shadows onto the for-est floor. Somewhere a whip-poor-will sang in the dark, delivering the slow, melodic and repetitive call that gave rise to its name. The whip-poor-will had the night to itself; other birds had gone silent. In early American folklore, a maiden would listen for the whip-poor-will. If it called but once, she had to wait a year to get married; two calls meant impending marriage. Three calls meant she had to wait three years. The insect-eating nocturnal bird is especially fond of moths. Its eggs are usually hatched around the time of full moon, allowing the parents the best opportunity to obtain food for their offspring. The larger chuck-will's-widow sounds much like a whip-poor-will and has many of the same habits; both species may be seen in Florida.

I love getting up in the morning, sitting by the fire with my eyes pointed east, waiting for the first glimmers of morning light. I was determined to make tracks before the heat rose, excited to see what the FT had in store alongside the Aucilla River. The path stayed on a land berm above the river, allowing vistas of the darkest of the blackwater rivers. Much smaller than the Suwannee, it averaged thirty to forty feet wide between banks about fifteen feet high, where palms, river birches, and oaks grew. Shade from overhanging branches gave the water an even darker aspect. Cypress grew along the water's edge, and the fast-moving Aucilla made watery sounds as it passed around the protruding cypress knees, creating white bubbles of froth. In places, limestone, eroded into sharp edges, provided a whitish contrast to the gloomy Aucilla.

The path sometimes dipped into ravines, where overflow swamps returned their waters to the river. Maples, holly and sparkleberry bushes bordered the trail, too, and the ever-present pines and saw palmettos found their places in this rich forest. Spiders had been busy at work overnight, stringing their webs. I kept having to peel back cobwebs from my face. Of course the spiders' intended fare was much smaller than a grown man. The Aucilla is prone to flooding, and when high, its dark waters stain the lowest parts of the tree trunks throughout the riverine woodland.

The Florida Trail reached Aucilla Rapids, a place where the river was constricted by rocks. I heard them well before I saw them. Forcing the entire flow between narrow walls of rock and trees created a rush of water louder than the rapids at my previous night's camp. The Aucilla is one of the Sunshine State's more challenging paddles, with such shoals as this.

The trail passed Burnt Bridge. Concrete abutments flanked the

Aucilla, and a long charred wood piling still stood tall in the river. Beyond Burnt Bridge came the first of the Aucilla Sinks. This is the point where canoeists have to take out as a series of sinks begins, windows in the limestone, where the river alternates between underground and surface flows. Here I could sometimes see the inflow at one end of the sink, then see where the outflow was at a limestone overhang where floating debris gathered at the water's edge, unable to flow underground to the next sink.

The trail followed the river as it did its disappearing-reappearing act. It created what you might call a series of ponds and short linear rivers, one of the strangest water/land features around. South of Goose Pasture Road the sinks increased in number. The eerily black water flowed from the land surface into the netherworld below, only to reappear in the nearby woods. You never could tell where it would come up next. Its odd character and propensity to head to the world below led me to call it the River Styx.

If you think about it, the Florida Trail was going over the river, around the river, and beside the river, but you never knew exactly where the trail was in relation to river, because innumerable other tiny sinks allowed only a slight glimpse of the Aucilla. Stranger still, each of these sinks had fish in it, catfish, bream, and more, swimming from one pond to the next. I ran into a fisherman in his chair beside a sink, spooning in a cold can of beans with car-greased hands while smoking a Marlboro. The blond pony-tailed and bearded angler, about thirty, told me he had fished twenty-seven of these sinks and had caught catfish in every one of them. I smelled gas on him. He must have been working on his aged red Japanese pickup, sitting in the distance. He had vowed to fish every sink, so he still had some hundreds to go.

The FT left the watery sinks and headed east away from the river, making a rocky track on public lands. These rich woods harbored the first dogwood I saw in bloom, its creamy white blossoms brightening an already bright day. Ahead was Powell Hammock Road. The sun burned stronger out here than in the shady woods. I headed south on

Powell Hammock Road, passing a dolomite mine, which was quiet this Sunday morning, as opposed to its normal loud operations. Dolomite is a soft rock similar to limestone and is used in fertilizers. All I heard was the scraping of my shoes against the hardened roadside dirt. Powell Hammock Road became paved. I could look ahead and see the heat shimmers running across the pavement. The cooking was on. I pushed through the shimmers.

Ahead, the FT followed U.S. Highway 98 west to bridge the Aucilla, which was flowing full for the nearby Gulf after emerging for good at Nutall Rise. It had gained the strong flow of the spring-fed Wacissa River. I stopped at JR's Aucilla Store and had a drink with the proprietor. He and his cronies inside were lamenting the sale and breakup of the timber lands around them, which were de facto game reserves. Now they were going to be "Yankee reserves," said one of the men. Another hoped the mosquitoes and 'gators would keep the intruders away. But that had been hoped for before, in now urbanized areas of the state. Change was happening even in the most inhospitable, hard-to-develop and remote areas of Florida like Taylor County. But if the Everglades could be turned into Miami International Airport, then anywhere in Florida can be turned into anything you can imagine building. At one time, most of Florida was inhospitable and remote. Then came the air conditioner, changing it from the most rural state in the South in 1900 to the most urban state in the South by the year 2000.

I left US 98 after it had bridged the deepest of sloughs and reentered woods in the Aucilla Wildlife Management Area, going from road walking to swamp slogging in a matter of feet. I sloshed through sun-warmed water, entering St. Marks National Wildlife Refuge. It had been a long-standing goal of mine to hike the FT through the refuge. This was an opportunity to hike one of the longest trails through any wildlife refuge in the United States. Now the time had come. Boardwalks crossed some wet land here, before the FT picked up an old logging tram road, elevated above the wooded swamp. The swamp hardwoods and palms, mixed with live oaks, were gorgeous here. Cypress and gum trees rose from the water amid exposed rock outcrops, quite unusual. The knees of cypress trees grew atop the tram road, lying in wait under the grass, ready to trip the unwary hiker.

I was getting tired and thus a candidate for a stumble. In St. Marks, camping is allowed only at designated backcountry sites. The next site was miles away. I was wishing to be farther along the trail, but I knew one thing about backpacking—you are never there until you are there. The track turned south and west, and the trail reached the main levee of the refuge, which was more open. The late afternoon light spilled perfectly onto pompous cedars with their pointed crowns, tall pines opening at the height of the forest, and green-topped palms, all casting shadowy patterns of dark and light upon the woodland floor.

A long wooden bridge spanned the Pinhook River, which was flowing out with the tide. I dropped my pack and went in for a dip. Crabs scattered at my feet. When I put my pants back on I noticed that the sheer motion of my legs moving had worn the crotch nearly bare.

A waft of pungent salt air drifted in from the Gulf, less than a mile to the south of me. Pinhook Campsite was just ahead. Clean now, I entered the official site to set up shop amid the pine-palm forest. It wasn't long before I was changing clothes to ward off the no-see-ums that were on the prowl. No-see-ums are tiny insects, also known as microjaws, or teeth with wings, that bite well out of proportion to their size. They are usually found along or near the coast but usually go away at dark. Where to I don't know; to sleep, I suppose. The mosquitoes took over the bugging at dusk, but that didn't detract from the appeal of this place as the moon rose over the Pinhook and a whip-poor-will provided dinner music for my noodle fare. I drifted off to sleep, whip-poor-will still repeating its sonorous sonata.

The first waft of warm air blew over the trail before the sun had even surmounted the horizon. I'd gotten an ultra-early start to beat the heat while I kept west on the old Aucilla Tram Road, as this was called. Shortly, the FT left the elevated roadbed and dipped into rich moist woods. The forest surface couldn't decide whether it was land or water; it was both. My shoes slipped and slid in the muck. The trailbed was nonexistent, due to too few walkers and excessive tree litter. Occasional orange blazes kept me confident of my route amid the live oaks, magnolias, bay trees, and maples, along with palms that grew tall enough to make me feel like a Lilliputian. The woodland was broken by thickets of cane and sawgrass. All this made for some of the roughest hiking this side of the Big Cypress. Ahead, many trees had blown down over the trail, likely courtesy of the hurricanes. I had to search for orange blazes amid the deadfall. If you were looking for the remote side of Florida, it was easily found here.

Wet feet didn't bother me as my shoes were already saturated from the day before. Dense black muck sucked at my feet, trying to pull off my shoes. I couldn't stop for long to admire the beauty of the soggy paradise, as the swamp angels would make me donate some blood as payment. Despite the early hour, sweat was pouring off me because of the strenuousness of hiking on ground that gave little resistance for pushing feet forward. In dry areas my feet crackled over dry palm fronds. Fallen trees forced continual detours. I imagined being a Florida aboriginal or a logger of yesteryear tramping through these swamps.

Miles of such tough travel led me back to the main levee, where a sign said: "Trail Closed—FT rerouted." I laughed, as the path I'd already trodden that day was closed for storm damage. The levee swung out toward the Gulf of Mexico, offering an elevated view of marsh lands broken with small palm islands. Tidal creeks cut through the marsh and views opened up for miles and miles and miles. I could even see the actual Big Bend of Florida, where the coast curved to the south, forming the state's peninsula. I thought about how the FT had navigated the peninsula amid all the state's residents.

The St. Mark's Lighthouse stood in the distance, a white cylindrical structure rising among the trees. Ahead, the levee simply gave way. The tide was rushing through the breach—more hurricane damage. Heavy storm rains had blown the levees wide open where the tides had once run through culverts. My whole hike was in effect an impromptu statewide storm damage walking tour, witness to the absolute power of a hurricane, or two or three, or more. This is my

Tidal creeks cut through the marsh and views opened for miles.

conclusion: after seeing what I have seen, if I were to find myself in an area that received an evacuation order, I'd be the first one out of town.

I walked down the broken soil of the levee and saw that it was possible to ford the moving water. Good thing it was low tide. This was also an opportunity to wash off the muck that had earlier splashed up my legs. Two more breaches in the dike lay ahead, the second of which was deep. A high incoming tide would have left me stranded. The hurricanes had visibly affected Florida, and the Florida Trail, everywhere my feet had led me.

The dike views kept on for miles. Palms grew in the foreground. Beyond, estuarine creeks extended out toward the Gulf, flowing amid sea grasses. Waterfowl impoundments stretched out on the landward side of the levee. Here, 'gators basked at the margins of land and water, while ducks and other winged creatures stayed clear of the reptiles.

Red-winged blackbirds flitted about in the grassy edges. The trail left the open marshes for freshwater wooded environs. I turned and went to the refuge headquarters to obtain a camping permit and pay a fee. The treated water from a fountain was admittedly good, better than the dark sulphur water of the swamp. While processing the permit I happily noticed a few of my guidebooks for sale in the visitor center. Seeing my books for sale in book stores or visitor centers of outdoor destinations, I'll admit, is always gratifying.

I rejoined the FT as it headed southwest for Port Leon, Florida's first railroad-accessible port. You probably haven't heard of it because it's a ghost town now, likely the state's first hurricane-devastated city. After Tallahassee was named Florida's capital, a twenty-two-mile rail line was built connecting Tallahassee to the Gulf near the mouth of the St. Marks River. Incorporated as the Wakulla county seat, the port town of Port Leon lasted but two years before a hurricane and tidal wave destroyed the community. It was never rebuilt.

At Port Leon I picked up the southernmost end of Florida's first railroad, which led north to the St. Marks River. The rail grade had a first-rate wilderness feel right until the moment it hit the St. Marks River. Across the way stood the quiet sea hamlet of St. Marks. No bridge here—hikers have to hail a boat to get across. I waited thirty minutes for a boat to pass. Along came a white sport-fishing boat containing two men. I called out, asking them for a ride. The two retired men were not happy about it. The captain motored toward the shore and said, "This is as far as I'm going." I waded out to thigh depth and then had raise myself from the water and climb onto the boat with brute arm force, which is tough when you are carrying a loaded backpack. The older man, the one not steering, sourly declared, "You should have brought a canoe."

"I'll just pull that out of my pack," I thought as I was apologizing for begging the ride. What was I to do? The driver boated me across to the dock of a restaurant. When about five feet from it he announced, "You better jump." My lower half was soaking, including of course my shoes, and I wasn't sure of the grip on the edge of the boat, but I went for it anyway, landing on the wooden dock and sending some startled shorebirds flying. I then had to walk right through the restaurant, which was nearly deserted.

The waitress offered me a glass of water as I passed through. This was getting surreal. I felt as if I were an inhabitant of Bob Dylan's "115th Dream," a song of his about one crazy episode after another. I drank from the proffered glass, standing with the pack on, water running down my legs, while the blonde waitress, about my age, smoked a cigarette. She had just moved there; from Jersey, I guessed by her accent. How she ended up in St. Marks I would never know. I thanked her for the water, handed her the empty glass, and headed down the street under a blazing sun, waiting for the next strange event.

I immediately went to Bo Lynn's, a country-style store in an old wooden building. I opened the squeaking front door. Inside it was dead quiet, and the wood creaked with my every footfall. An ancient woman, thin as a rail, with long white hair and no teeth, sat behind the counter with a man I took to be her son. Both mindlessly followed me with their eyes as I moved around. I was just something new to look at. It was your classic country store, dark, with goods lining the shelves in less than logical order. My eyes adjusted to the light. I was not seeing things: their prices really were that high, especially for batteries. I grabbed a few things anyway, succumbing to the convenience, and headed back into the light.

A well-dressed middle-aged couple stood outside the store, and the man asked where I was headed. He knew I was hiking the Florida Trail. We discussed our fondness for St. Marks Refuge and the Florida outdoors in general. I walked on, thinking how normal that encounter was. Now I would pick up the Tallahassee–St. Marks Historic Railroad State Trail, a mouthful of a name for the northbound continuation of the railroad grade the FT had followed from Port Leon, south of the St. Marks River. On this side, however, the trail was paved and mown and a popular recreation destination. I sweatily followed the rail trail to US 98, then got a gallon of water from a new-fashioned convenience store. The FT headed west, where it paralleled US 98. I found a campsite in some pines off the road, glad to be ending this twenty-mile day, and got set for a night of rain, the first in sixteen days.

Big white clouds rolled in as I picked the first of ten ticks off me. Some were tiny, some larger. You just pull with your fingers as close as you can to where they are biting. The clouds merged into one massive blanket. However, no rain fell during the stifling night as I sweltered under the bug netting, haphazardly rigged under the tiny tarp. A claustrophobic person would have gone crazy in the tiny enclosure, but I summoned up my powers of sleeping and forced it to happen. At 5:00 a.m. the humidity and closeness ran me out for fresh air, so I crawled out of the rain-, bug-, and breeze-proof setup to make a little coffee and watch the day break. Overhead, the clouds said rain to me. I didn't need a weatherman for what was above me, but what was at ground level on the Florida Trail was unknown.

16

The Nexus of Land and Sea

I altered the plan, leaving my stuff to head back toward St. Marks and hit the Dollar General. Their batteries were cheap. I quickly blew through the store, anxious to get outside again, even if it was hot. I love real air, be it hot, cold, wet or dry, instead of vent-driven air circulating inside a building shut tight. Back at camp I crammed the new stuff into the pack under a darkening sky, then took off. Rain was coming. The sky blackened and the wind whirled, but I ignored it. Just east of the Wakulla River the rain hit, riding a blast of wind, making it difficult to secure the poncho over myself and the pack.

I was back in the St. Marks Refuge, aiming for the coast, and sure to wet my dogs again. The selling point of the shoes I wore was their ability to drain water out after walking through water. However, this feature also allowed rain or any other water to flow in. The light shower mandated keeping the poncho on, despite feeling as if I was a saran-wrapped burrito in a microwave oven. I entered a thick pine forest with high brush, winding amid tall evergreens under a blank gray sky. The woodland's look of sameness with no sun to aid my direction led me to feel as if the trail was traveling in circles. But it wasn't, and I crossed a fence line.

The woods changed to a mix of pines and oaks. I passed a huge old sawdust pile called Sawdust Hill, a relic from a long ago logging mill; the sawdust pile was the only obvious evidence. The nearby woods told no tale either. They were completely regrown. The forest floor tilted to swamp, and spring reigned: the deciduous trees seemed to be greening before my eyes, that electric green that a drab gray winter makes you forget is possible. The rain stopped and the trees stopped dripping too, but the trail wet me to mid-shin—from the ground up, walking through water.

At times I had my doubts about hiking. What was the purpose? Why take this long route through wet, albeit beautiful, woods? Why not just stay on dry and certain US 98? But in the same vein, why not just drive from Big Cypress to Alabama in one day? Why not just watch *Florida Trail: The Video*? I took the long way because the long way was the rewarding way. It took effort and a time investment. You earn every mile on the trail. And hiking is the only way to see places like The Cathedral, where tall palms reached upward to create a continuous frond canopy—a roof that could be likened to the grace of a church, a place you had to walk to see, get your feet wet to feel, a place where your feet squished as you marveled, a place so still and so silent as to mock the hurried highways of the world.

Ahead, a spur trail led to Shepherd Spring. This silent upwelling pool is among the massive springs of Florida, wider than a house, encircled by woods. An outflow headed for the Gulf. Gar fish floated motionless in the water as I dipped my bottle into the blue aqua. What a treat to drink this after all the swamp water I'd been ingesting. Perhaps this is why you take the long hard route, to see a spring in its natural state, completely undeveloped, requiring miles on foot to see it.

Fiddleheads were rising in damp spots along the trail, soon to unfurl into bright green ferns. The path rose to drier land, where longleaf pines stood tall amid waist-high brush. Some of this brush was blooming pink. The wild azalea blooms much more delicately than cultivated ones. Unpruned and untamed, spindly at the bottom and rising to open blooms resting on fragile arms, the wild azalea didn't have to knock you over with numbers. Its colorful presence veritably lit up the woods and needed no aid from us.

The Florida Trail climbed away from a place called Wakulla Fields and rode high dry pine country, making for easier hiking at the end of a long day. The clouds had passed east, letting the sun shine on St. Marks. Temperatures in the thirties were predicted, so near State Road 365 I found some woods on private land near the trail to make camp. Fires are not allowed on the refuge. The mercury didn't drop as much as predicted, but I did dry my shoes and socks before the flames, planning on dry feet for the next day.

The cool clear morning was welcome as I followed the FT over bridged wetlands between dry woods. It seemed the trail was actively avoiding wet areas, for once. Before, the land had been more wet than dry, leaving wet options as the only options. The trail was not in any hurry to leave the refuge and sought scenic locales, such as Marsh Point. The forest changed from minute to minute with elevation. I went through the Bridges, where swamp strands of water-loving plants divided drier woods. The area morphed from one ecosystem to another: dry scrub oaks to palm–live oak woods to cypress strands. St. Marks claims more ecosystems than any other area in North Florida.

The FT angled for the Gulf and curved along the margin where the forested land met the cordgrass marshes of the coast. Small palm islands stood amid the cordgrass. I smelled salt in the air. During the Civil War, the Confederates had salt-making operations around here. Salt was an important commodity back then—it was used as a food preservative. Armies of thousands of men need transportable food. At the beginning of the war, salt prices shot up, leading to these operations. In those years this was the back of beyond. Even so, the crude salt-drying ponds were protected by soldiers. It is said you can still discern the circular pond outlines in the cordgrass. Ocean debris had overwashed onto the land here.

Marsh Point offered a 180-degree view of the nexus of land and sea, where cedars, palms, and oaks formed a thick border to the cordgrass, which in turn bordered the salt marsh creeks that flowed to the Gulf, in and out, with the cycles of the moon. The FT left Marsh Point. This was as close as I'd get to the ocean for the duration of the hike. Ahead, some brand new boardwalks had been installed by spring breakers from Michigan, a park volunteer told me. The FT had formerly run along Purify Bay Road but had now been rerouted to woods, just another moment of maturation of the trail. It changed again, rising to a hill thick with turkey oaks. Here the deciduous trees were budding out with lime green leaves, sure to darken and subdue with time. I reached US Highway 319 and the end of the refuge portion of the FT and felt the satisfaction that comes with fulfilling an ambition one has carried around for a while. Now I had seen this coastal refuge. Another long unbroken stretch of foot trail lay just across US 319.

17

Created by the Forces of Nature

Entering the Apalachicola National Forest, I stopped at the trail register at the beginning of this trail section, and in the registry box I found a copy of a page from my book *Long Trails of the Southeast*. This page described the section I was about to hike. I put it in my pocket, after reading the description. Obviously, I had hiked the FT through the Apalachicola National Forest several times, but I looked forward to hiking it again. It is beautiful, challenging, and unforgiving. It is nature for nature's sake.

Titi, a bush that loves wetlands, and thus loves Florida, was blooming its thousands of white blossoms, growing upwards of thirty feet high along streambeds, and was green with leaves, too. The surrounding pine woods had recently been burned; they wore shades of brown, copper, and black and smelled burned. I covered two miles in the national forest before making camp just beyond a creek spanned by a plank walkway. The area near the creek wasn't burned, enhancing its campability. I sat in the creekside grass and absorbed this gorgeous sunny day. It could only be lived once.

As I was puffing on a cigar, noises came from the creek. Someone—several someones—were coming over the plank walkway. They were talking but I couldn't understand the words. A middle-aged man in a national forest uniform and a big straw hat walked into the sun. He spotted my creek-rinsed clothes and hat drying in the sun and walked over to them. I sat silently, twenty feet away in plain sight, blowing smoke and waiting. The ranger gave the duds a closer inspection, then turned around and saw me. He said, "I knew you had to be close. No man leaves his hat far behind."

I laughed, then stood up and introduced myself to him and his compadres, two rangerettes also in uniform, all trying to get out of the office on a day like this. They were inspecting "user-created" roads; that is, roads people had made by driving through the woods. The crew dressed in green went on with their inspection, leaving me on my own to watch the sun setting. After dark, coyote pups howled beyond the campfire, adding an eerie aspect to this moonlit night.

My shoes were falling apart after sixty days. The heels were devoid of cushioning, which is always the demise of the low-top lightweight hiking shoes I prefer. The heel-on-hard-plastic interaction was in danger of becoming a pain in the foot. I'd gotten eight hundred miles out of these shoes and they had cost eighty dollars, so I figured ten cents per mile was well worth it. I had already called my reliable Johnson City friend Lynnette Barker, who had gone over to my house and fished up a certain pair of hiking shoes and was mailing them to Bristol. But Bristol was still seventy miles from here.

The sun hit quick in this open pine country. The recent forest burn had cleared the understory, giving the sun more places to shine. Burn lines ended at the thickets of titi, which grew in tangled profusion. The fresh burn also obscured the orange blazes and made the footbed less visible and harder to follow. As the FT headed into pine-palmetto woods, the early morning sun backlit the palmettos, giving them a bright appearance, as if each were plugged into an unseen electrical outlet. The smell of sun-warmed pine needles wafted through the cool morning air. I looked up and marveled in the colors of a crystal blue sky contrasting against the white sand track speckled with bronze needles. The picture seemed to call out for an artist and palette. I was glad to be alive and on the Florida Trail. And my feet weren't even hurting, despite the state of my shoes. Chalk it up to outlook: I choose to define myself by my strengths and accomplishments, rather than my failures and weaknesses, and I fully expected to finish the trail. I am a finisher.

I came to the Sopchoppy and crossed a concrete bridge, which had replaced a quaint but probably unsafe wooden one. Ahead, the FT cruised along the west bank of the Sopchoppy on some of the hilliest terrain this side of the Suwannee River, dipping down to ravines, some of which were bridged. The trail then left the river to work toward a crossing of Monkey Creek, a major stream feeding the Sopchoppy. The bridge had been out for a while and was now on its side, pushed against a tree by some flood. I could nevertheless use the wooden structure to make it far enough across to jump the rest of the way, though the creek was low enough to ford. A bridge has since been installed there. Monkey Creek's lowness meant that Bradwell Bay and its renowned swamp tromp would be low as well. The trail returned to the Sopchoppy, a river I had not only walked across before but had paddled.

I harkened back to the first time I'd canoed it, my first Florida river. Childhood friend Wes Shepherd and I had driven five hundred miles to the town of Sopchoppy, intending to rent a canoe from an outfitter. But the outfitter had gone out of business. We drove around town, hoping we might yet find the business, though we suspected the truth. I spotted a decrepit canoe against the side of a decrepit wood house, stopped, and knocked on the door; I was the one who had pushed for this canoe trip. A big-gutted bald man with a six-day beard answered the door. Yes, he would rent out the canoe for twenty bucks. "Make sure it floats," was the last thing he said as he closed the creaking door. We then found a guy with a truck at the local convenience store and paid him to take us upriver. And down the Sopchoppy we went, spending three nights on the river—black water, sandbars, cypress knees, sitting by a fire, sand under our feet, shirtless, watching a baited pole, waiting for a fish to bite . . .

Pink azaleas bloomed along the river and in the adjoining woods, just as they had that first canoe trip. I reached another bridge, then turned left on a forest road to reach the Bradwell Bay Wilderness trailhead. I entered the fabled wilderness, widely regarded as Florida's toughest hiking experience. The first few miles, however, were easy, as they traced an old forest road through open land. The sun grew fierce and the afternoon temperature was approaching 80 degrees. The relentless sun was my enemy in this scrubby area, and I recalled more of that trip with Wes. We had returned the canoe—which did float—to the surprised man, who probably figured he had gotten his canoe hauled off and been paid twenty bucks to boot. We then decided to backpack along the Sopchoppy. The Florida Trail ran beside it; we had seen the blazes from the water and checked it out. This had also been my first backpacking trip in Florida. We had taken the Florida Trail north from this very trailhead and had planned to camp on the river and do some more bank fishing. Unbeknownst to us, however, was that when you go north from this trailhead, the FT never gets near the river. It leaves the Sopchoppy for good near the trailhead. We ended up hacking a campsite out of trailside brush in some open pines, carrying purposeless fishing rods. Wes never trusted my woodsmanship after that.

Ahead, the FT turned west off the old forest road Wes and I had followed. In the distance I could see the white-topped cloudlike titi thickets. I knew water was ahead and swamp slogging was imminent. The trailside brush was high, but not high enough for shade—only high enough to scratch my legs. The sun beat overhead. A few fire-scarred pines stood above the brush. Most had fallen in skewed patterns, as if someone had dropped a giant box of matchsticks. The whole place had a raw, rough look to it. Waves of heat rose and shimmered in the distance on the palmetto prairies, bordered by the titi thickets, where water flowed. Places like this were created solely by the forces of nature—lightning, sun, wind, and rain—each sculpting the landscape in its own way.

"Another day of not seeing a human being," I said out loud. It simply was what it was—solitude. At the camp I dubbed The Oaks, located just east of the serious foot wetting, a dozen or so scrub live oaks grew, patching together a bit of shade on level land with a light grassy floor, as opposed to the dense brush that covered the rest of what little dry land was around. I got water from a tea-colored creek, where the remnants of an old bridge, just some squared off logs, sat silent, forming a pool as they backed up the nameless creek washing over them. I washed off and waited for the evening cool down.

But the weather rollercoaster wouldn't go down. I lay still underneath the netting, listening to mosquitoes buzz under the cloudy sky.

Restless sleep was broken by a late rising moon. The cloud cover diffused the light, making it seem as if dawn had arrived though it was only 2:30 a.m.

The dark morning made the area seemed more foreboding as I left The Oaks and went deeper into Bradwell Bay Wilderness, crossing burned-over wet forests open to the dark sky. A misty drizzle increased the gloom. I had hiked this part of the FT the year before, and the hurricanes had done their best to knock over all the dead trees still standing after an earlier forest fire. Now I reached the full-blown swamp, the heart of Bradwell Bay, named for a hunter of yesteryear who got lost and went around in circles for days, slogging through ancient swamp forests, ragged pine lands, and the snakelike titi thickets. It was darker than dusk in the swamp, under the tree canopy of gum, cypress, pine, and other trees. The water looked black as I felt my way forward, testing the swamp bottom with each step, expecting to go in up to my thighs, and sometimes I would, even when the previous ten steps had held me up fine. It was the nature of this swamp and the reason for its notorious reputation.

The tortuously twisted branches of the titi grew close to the path. As I passed by, my motion sent titi blooms—tiny white petals—dropping onto the black water, floating like a thousand junks in the bays of Hong Kong, eventually to soak, sink, and rot, adding another layer to the muck beneath. I made Bradwell Island, a small dry pineland, yet the swamp gave no quarter, and the Florida Trail returned me to the slow depths where ancient trees towered in strength, as if laughing at a land-bound passerby attempting to navigate the waters where they thrived. Some places that were normally underwater were mud, good pig- sloppin' mud, in some ways more challenging than walking through water. The mud clung to my shoes, socks, and legs, making me feel as if I was hiking in with leg irons.

I came to moving water. It's strange to see moving water in a swamp, but swamps have their own drainage patterns. The deepest part was just ahead, and where the biggest trees were still getting bigger. These ancients did not know dry land and likely never would. I picked my way forward, plunging deeper, then broke on through to the other

Places that were normally underwater were mud, in some ways more challenging than walking through water.

side, reaching a hellish area—still in mucky and sometimes murky water but open to the sky, with fallen burned trees everywhere, a result of a fire followed by hurricane. Every now and then I would find a blaze on a fallen tree and proceed on, then realize I had moved off course and start hunting for the next blaze. Finally I picked up an old logging berm that was dry. Whew! A couple more wet areas loomed, including a long narrow water walk that had once been a road. My reward for escaping the swamp was to see a blooming pitcher plant just beyond the final slog.

And just like that I popped out on Forest Road 314, a little blacker, a lot dirtier, and carrying half my body weight in shoe muck. But Bradwell Bay was behind me. The trail went on and off old forest roads and through wet pine plantations to emerge onto paved County Road 375, four miles from Bradwell Bay. I took a side trail to the Langston Homestead, an old homesite. The dilapidated wooden structure shaded by massive live oaks was falling apart. Azaleas still bloomed in the yard, forgetting that no one lived there to enjoy them. The tin roof had been peeled back like the top of a sardine can, no doubt by wind.

I walked a trail to the backyard and a boxed-in spring that served the Langstons. It was full of leaves and useless for drinking. Graveled paths and other evidence showed that the U.S. Forest Service had at one point made a start on using the place as an interpretive site, but the project had been abandoned. I peered inside the house, seeing a musty collection of cobwebs. Someone had called this home. When seeing abandoned houses I always wonder about the last person who spent the last night inside. Did whoever it was know that was the end?

I left Langston and went on up the paved CR 375. The FT left the road and entered private land, where it traced an old roadbed down to a clear stream, then curved to bluffs along big Ochlockonee River, ultimately within sight of it. Beech trees, with their smooth mottled gray bark, grew along the bluff line, but magnolias dominated the rich forest. The trail crossed a clear cool spring seep and I stopped for lunch. The sun burned off the clouds as I ate yet another lunch of peanut butter and blueberry preserves. The heat came right behind the departing cloud as I road walked across the bridge spanning the Ochlockonee River and its shoulder swamps.

At Porter Lake Campground the trail dipped back into woods. I was losing momentum and looking to make camp, but the campground was along a road and therefore a no-go. The trail crossed one more forest road and put me in a potential camping zone. The first creek bottom I reached was too low and mushy, but the second had more potential, especially viewed with tired eyes. The land rose from the creek and I found a camp in the margin where the titi met the pines, a level open spot in the shade of the titi bushes. I craved shade. I returned to the creek to wash off the grime and rinse out my shoes and socks, still full of muck and sand from the Bradwell Bay crossing.

This time of day was always welcome. I had completed the day's mileage and was clean. Next I would look in the pack to see what I could eat, simultaneously filling the gut and lightening the load. Then came a map check to sketch out the next day roughly. Finally I would lie back and watch the sun dip lower, make a fire, and have some coffee as soon as the evening was cool enough. I sat still, half slumped against the pack, head still high enough to slurp coffee, watching mosquitoes maneuver around, seeking uncovered skin, drifting into my ears and onto my pants. I was covered in a long-sleeved shirt and long pants, with socks and bug dope on exposed skin. They weren't bad; just around and needing to be dealt with. I had to admire the persistence of mosquitoes. They never gave up in their quest for blood. If more of us had this persistence, we would more successfully reach our goals.

The sun shot a few last rays between the pines, as if not wanting to relinquish its influence over these remote Florida woods. Crickets whirred in time, cycling through their simple song. The wind stilled and the smoke from the small fire moved as slowly as I did. Dusk was just down the trail, waiting to move in. The lightning bugs were following behind.

My throat was threatening to close up from disuse. No conversation. I had seen people in cars along CR 375 that day, but the only interaction had been a brief wave in the country fashion as they drove by. No words. This was solitude at its finest, if you like solitude.

The next day's trail segment would be the shortest, driest route amid the pine mounds divided by titi thickets and swamp trees, but that didn't mean the route was either short or dry. I walked through a nasty burned thicket where I had black branches tattooing my arms. A flat of mud looked crossable, but I ended up stuck in muck up to my knee and nearly yanked off a shoe trying to pull my leg out. I made Vilas, an old turpentine town that had been abandoned. All that was left were old fences and concrete and rock piles. The trail spanned the New River on a bridge, then went upstream along it. Atlantic white cedars grew along this watercourse and along most streams from here heading west. The evergreen trunks grew straight, not necessarily straight for the sky, but whatever angle they took, they kept a solid direction. On higher ground, buddied up with the pines, were the turkey oaks. At this stage their leaves were an impossible shade of yellowy green, such as you would see in a lava lamp. The pines ringed in white paint were red-cockaded woodpecker nesting trees—the forest service cut brush and grass low around these trees to prevent them from catching fire during prescribed burns.

I stopped near Hostage Branch to make camp. The water was low throughout the forest, and that was troublesome. Most of the creeks I had crossed had had flowing water, but it was separated from campable dry pineland by long stretches of mud trail that I would have had to negotiate to get water. Hostage Branch was spanned by a forest road, forcing the water through a culvert and making it easier to get. Culvert water was no problem for me. Culverts often act as fountains when the water pours out of them. I was a hostage to water, though the best spots to lay my head were in the high dry pines. That day I saw no people, no cars, though I had crossed a couple of roads. I was in a large national forest with few people living nearby, which added up to a lot of land and few bodies. In times of solitude like this, my simple hiking existence seemed utterly disconnected from the rest of the world, even my own world back home, as if home were something I dreamed up. The Florida Trail was life itself.

Since Tina had left, I had upped the hiking miles. Thus my appetite had increased just as the quality of the fare had decreased. For filler, I was adding instant mashed potatoes to my noodle dinners. Talk about a starchy supper! The concoction had the consistency of spackling—dense, white and heavy, puttylike. I chewed it like a cow chews its cud, washing it down with a hefty helping of gen-u-ine Florida swamp water.

I left Hostage Branch ready for an easy morning cruise. But ahead, the trail was overgrown and scratchy and wet—another surprise from the Florida Trail. This was my payback, apparently, for the recently cleared trail in other parts of the Apalachicola National Forest. Titi had spread over the path, leaving a narrow corridor barely kept open by hikers. Burned titi was now crusted in black soot, which, if it didn't cut me, painted stripes on me. Gnarly defined this section. But let me be clear: despite the troubles, I loved the Apalachicola. It was no walk in the park, not the spot for a mother-daughter stroll down a groomed path in matching outfits, flowers tucked into hair, sun glinting through manicured trees. The Apalachicola simply was and didn't care if you walked through it or not.

The forest had its offerings. Pink azaleas brightened the morning woods. The morning sun did glint through the trees, sometimes illuminating a titi branch so heavy with tiny white blooms that it hung to the ground. Several long boardwalks wound through Shuler Bay, where red and green blooming pitcher plants bordered grassy seeps. The path opened and became easy, and I reached the junction with the Trail of Lakes. Bonnet Pond, ringed in cypress and dotted with lily pads, lured me for a stop. The FT then cruised flats where dogwoods bloomed amid an army of turkey oaks. A burned area sprouted baby turkey oaks, all with delicate yellow-green leaves, their foliage emerging ahead of that on full-sized turkey oaks above them. The small ones leaf out early to beat the shading by their larger brethren. I cruised by revamped Camel Lake campground and deposited some trash. Lightening the load is always a plus for a long-distance hiker. A bonus was a water spigot, from which I chugged before filling up the bottle.

The terrain grew hillier beyond Camel Lake, the trail then reaching an ecosystem known as pine savannas. Grassy meadows were pocked with buttress-based pine trees, to withstand the regular inundating of the savannas, which were wet more often than not. Pitcher plants grew here in incredible numbers. The footbed was extremely lumpy, raising the possibility of twisting an ankle. Some spots were lumpy and muddy, but the trail was a lot drier than in some sections I'd covered. Other wildflowers complemented the pitcher plants. Amid all this were ant hills rising from the grasses. Some were taller than they were high—ant condos. The hardworking ants used the grass of the savannas as a framework for building their mud homes. The last open grassy area brought me to Liberty County Road 12.

Now I left behind the Apalachicola National Forest and the swamplands of the last hundred plus miles. I turned north on CR 12 with the sun at my back, aiming for Bristol, hoping I had a package waiting.

18

Sole Searching

The trudge up County Road 12 was long and hot. I stopped briefly near a field, placing my pack against a telephone pole, and began rummaging through the pack for a snack, when suddenly I was getting bitten like crazy. Bugs by the hundreds were eating up my legs. I turned to find that upwards of twenty cows had eased over to the fence to check on their visitor in hope that I had a treat for them. Instead, they brought the mosquitoes over for a treat—me! I hastily reloaded and proceeded on, reaching Lake Mystic.

As I sat on a shady bench slurping a cold drink, up came a fellow about my age, wearing blue-jean short pants, to get a newspaper. The box was right next to me. I looked up and smiled, and in his instantaneous assessment he must have determined I was okay. He asked, "Where have you been?" I told him I had just hiked the entirety of the Apalachicola National Forest. He said, "That explains the scratches on your legs." I looked down. My legs were bad. Red stripes criss-crossed my thighs and shins, looking like a road map to the local blood donor center. I went on, telling him I'd actually hiked from near Miami and that the Florida Trail went right through his town. He knew the FT was in the national forest, but his eyes widened in surprise at the idea that it also came through the town.

In the afternoon I was still heading up CR 12. Just as roadside oranges fell off trucks in the orange country hundreds of miles back, around Orlando, here bark aplenty lay on the roadsides, from log trucks servicing the vast pinelands. People were sitting out on their porches, watching the guy walking up the road with the backpack. I'd wave and smile. They would wave back.

I made Bristol and the end of CR 12. Having bought some grub, I walked west toward the Apalachicola River to find a place for a "hobo camp" near town. Since it was Sunday, I had wait for the morning to go to the post office. I found the ideal spot in some level oak woods beside a seeded field with a hunting blind. Of course, in a hobo camp near town, instead of birds you hear the sounds of cars and trains, and instead of twinkling stars, you get twinkling cell phone towers.

I made my fire small so as not to attract attention and slept well that night, getting up at 5:00 a.m. in anticipation of the long day ahead. I lit a morning fire and sat drinking coffee in the dark. Suddenly, headlights appeared on the road leading to my camp. Uh-oh. The car stopped as close as it could get to my camp, about fifty feet distant. The silence after the engine stopped was deafening. I helplessly moved between the auto and the flames, futilely hoping to block the firelight. The headlights went off, the door opened, and then the door closed. Here was my nightmare—camping on private property, I was about to get into trouble.

I backed up, letting the fire show me to my visitor and make me as unthreatening as possible. The figure walked toward me. Then a man's deep voice calmly asked, "Who are you?" I nervously identified myself then went into my hiking-the-Florida-Trail spiel. The man, about my age, came up to the fire, and I could see him in the dim light. He had on a work shirt with a name, jeans, and work boots. "I've heard of the Florida Trail," he said. Alright, I thought; most people in Florida haven't. Next I explained about the package, and that as the day before had been Sunday, I was now fixing to break camp and head for the post office.

The man was interested in the hike, and I told him all about it. The atmosphere relaxed as he picked up a twig to stoke the fire, and he told me he was up here to listen for turkeys. Ah, a hunter. As dawn broke our conversation became downright friendly because Alvin Foran is a friendly fellow, a Bristol native. Alvin and I discussed turkeys, hunting, fishing, how beautiful the spring was, and the different wildflowers we had seen. Clearly Alvin and I shared a love of and appreciation for his neck of the woods. I broke camp as we talked, and he offered to drive me to the post office. I accepted, after stashing my pack in the woods. You never know what kind of person you may meet in the dark woods outside a town. It just might be a new friend.

I waited outside for the post office to open. An ancient man tottered up to check his box. Emerging from the lobby empty-handed, he stopped, looked at me, and declared, "Useless trip." I hoped that wasn't a bad omen. The postmistress came out to raise our nation's flag, and she greeted me. I told her I was a Florida Trail thru-hiker waiting for a package. She said, "I saw it just a minute ago. I'll get it for you." Yes! Lynnette and the post office had come through. Along with the shoes, Lynnette had thrown in a giant chocolate candy bar, which I consumed on the spot.

The old shoes went unceremoniously into the dumpster next door and off I went, westward across the Apalachicola River, with a new spring in my step and a new time zone through which to walk. The swamp woods below the bridge were wearing their spring greens, bordering the mud-stained Apalachicola. At the high point of the bridge I could see far to the north, but I was going west, deeper into the Panhandle, and westward on the Florida Trail.

19

Living on Central Time

Luckily, the bridge over the Apalachicola River had a pedestrian walk-way, as it was one and a half miles of bridge, then more bridges over swamps bordering the river. I was back on terra firma and headed into Blountstown. It was Bristol's cross-river twin, so to speak; pure South. I was going to resupply and wash my dirty clothes, which had seen only creek rinsings for the past two weeks. As I neared Blount-stown's old courthouse—one of the most beautiful in Florida, red brick surrounded by palm trees—a white pickup truck slowed down. I looked over to see the fellow who had chatted with me at the Lake Mystic grocery. He asked if I wanted to eat breakfast.

I power-walked through town and then tossed my pack into the bed of his truck as I headed into Connie's, our appointed meeting place. I sweatily joined him and his daughter Hannah, learning both her name and his—Rex. After cooling down in the air conditioning, I told Rex about my encounter with Alvin earlier in the morning. I should not have been surprised when it turned out he knew Al-vin; Bristol, Florida, is a small world. I enjoyed the hearty breakfast and good company. The father and daughter followed me over to the laundromat, where before starting the wash, I showed dark-haired Hannah my portable computer and how to type on its collapsible keyboard.

We said goodbye. I was thinking about how easily I had made a few friends in these friendly parts when up came a young reporter from the county paper to do a story on me. She was full of pep and zing for the hike and for the FT going through Blountstown. It turned out that Rex had dropped in at the newspaper office on his way home, knowing I was more or less captive for a while at the laundry. The reporter knew Rex's wife, of course. As the laundry proceeded through its cycles, I also befriended some retired New Yorkers down on a vacation. They had overheard the interaction with the reporter and told me about their adventurous son, who also liked the outdoors. Then a woman named Christina, with her three boisterous offspring, quizzed me further, having overheard all the preceding conversation. The laundromat errand was providing a great opportunity to promote the Florida Trail and to interact with people who live along it.

I asked Christina to watch my pack while I went next door to the Piggly Wiggly to resupply. I didn't worry about the computer or the camera or anything else in the pack. Having known the thirty-ish brown-eyed mother with the short haircut for all of one hour, I simply trusted Christina. She delivered her viewpoints with conviction. Her confidence won me over. I love confident people operating from a set of principles. What a far cry from my first trip into the grocery store in Clewiston, when I carried my valuables in my pocket while shopping. It's great trusting in people. I'd rather do that and get burned every now and then than not be able to trust fellow citizens. I brought back some ice cream sandwiches for us and her offspring.

I finished my laundry and said goodbye to Christina. Then I was on my way, heading into the hot afternoon with a long road walk and a heavy pack but a light heart buoyed by the encouragement and enthusiasm of my newfound coterie of friends. Solitude has benefits, but friends do, too. They all were in the adventure and could, would, and should share in its success. The road walk gave me plenty of time to reflect on "Make a New Friend Day" in Calhoun County. Despite the heat, I cranked out the fourteen miles to reach the Chipola River. The sun was getting low as I followed a sandy road along the river and found a campsite. I stripped and went swimming in the green waters of the Chipola, washing away the sweat and grime of the past few days. Now I had clean clothes and a clean body.

The night stayed stiflingly hot and the swamp angels buzzed around my netting. The weather radio said Calhoun County and a few others nearby were under a tornado watch. A line of storms was headed my way. I set up that pathetic poncho/tarp, laughing at the prospect of being under it during a tornado. Battening down the hatches as best I could, I draped the netting over me and laid myself to rest, waiting to be awakened by the overnight squall. The heat was so thick that I never got into the sleeping bag. Rain came, but it was light, and the wind was far from tornadic.

Dawn arrived. I had been spared the storm. It had moved farther north, mainly into Alabama. The Great Weather Card Dealer had handed me a royal flush. I left the Chipola under dark clouds, however, and shortly got popped by a heavy shower. Shelton's Store was nearby, so I went in to get a cup of coffee and shot the bull with the middle-aged proprietor. He said FT hikers came through "every now and then." I asked him if the Yankees were moving into Florida. I'll never forget his reply. He leaned back in his chair behind the register, hesitated with good effect, and said with emphasis, "*Everybody* is moving to Florida."

I went west, replaying the conversation, still on CR 274, thinking how we needed to get this Florida Trail fully established as a protected corridor from end to end before everyone did move here. I kept rolling, now in sand hill country, where widely spaced sand pines and turkey oaks covered high hills between thicker woods along the meandering streams. The heat hung tough and the sun broke out. Steam rose from everything wet, including me. I was near melting, dissolving into liquid like a chocolate bar left on a car dashboard in August. I pushed on, making it to public lands astride Econfina Creek. The Florida Trail led for a mile through sun-splashed young pines with needles twisting in a hot wind. The path mercifully entered shady woods before reaching Econfina Creek.

This was the Econfina Creek of Washington County, as opposed to the Econfina River of Taylor County, along which the Florida Trail also ran. Both rivers are fine canoeing destinations. The lands along this creek were owned and managed by Northwest Florida Water Management District. Much of Panama City gets its drinking water from this watercourse and its springs and tributaries, dammed downstream as Deer Point Lake. Small creeks cut ravines toward the river.

Giant magnolias, oaks, and smooth-barked beech trees bordered the pathway. Sparkleberry, mountain laurel, and azaleas formed a dense understory. Tall pines towered here and there.

I stumbled into a campsite overlooking the creek and dropped my pack. The bluff offered a fine view of the waterway below. It was mere moments before I was in the river, dunking myself. Relief. I felt like a new man and made camp. A small spring emerged from a rocky bank nearby. The water was cool and clear, no flavoring required. Things were looking up. Panama City, the nearest reporting station to my location, set a record high that day. Night came on and the human world was silent in this deep valley protected by wild lands on all sides. There were only the noises of the wild: an owl downstream, coyotes on the hill, and something I couldn't see was rummaging through the leaves across the creek; probably an armadillo.

Cool air filtered in before down. The front behind the storm was arriving. I had the customary fire and coffee. While breaking camp I was treated to dueling woodpeckers. Woodpecker A would knock on a tree, *whap-whap-whap-whap* in rapid-fire succession, then woodpecker B would follow. I imagined an insect-eating contest, but perhaps they did this early every morning. The clear, cool sunny morn contrasted greatly with the dark, warm, and stormy start of the day before. Along the trail the vegetation was so tight that I had to twist and turn my backpack to wrangle amid the tightly growing holly, sparkleberry, azaleas, and mountain laurel. Red cardinals twittered in the brush, the bright males outdoing the more subdued brownish females.

The FT led me down Econfina Creek, spanning it twice on bridges, and other bridges spanned feeder streams. The narrow trail was more than just a scenic respite from the road walk of the day before. This, in my opinion, was the most scenic stretch of the entire Florida Trail. The creek itself was beautiful, with its banks of dripping ferns, occasionally opening to sandbars. Trees overhung the waterway, where sandy shallows contrasted with darker, deeper sections. Limestone walls reflected the morning sunlight. Cane thrived in the ravines.

One feeder branch offered a waterfall. It flowed off a hillside and

The FT led me down Econfina Creek, spanning it twice on bridges.

over the lip of a limestone wall into the Econfina, making quite a splash. The feeder branches were flowing swiftly, crystal clear—well, perhaps not *crystal* clear, but a darn sight more drinkable than the waters of the nearly stagnant swamplands through which I'd been passing. As American outdoorsman go, I consider myself quite the connoisseur of wilderness water, and I rated the branches of the Econfina among the finest drinking waters in the Sunshine State. Here I could use my mountain water method of drinking: dip-and-sip—just dip the water bottle and sip away. The usual method in much of Florida was dip-flavor-chug. I'd dip the water bottle in, flavor the water with a drink packet, and then chug it down before I got either a good taste or a good look.

As good as it tastes, the Econfina is even better for canoeing. With a gradient of nine feet per mile—unheard of elsewhere in Florida— the Econfina plunges down its little gorge, twisting and turning, requiring paddlers to use stop-on-a-dime turns and good maneuvering skills to dodge fallen trees. The fishing wasn't bad, either. I had canoe camped in this valley and was now privileged to be backpacking it, too. The Econfina is truly a jewel of the Panhandle.

The FT held more surprises as it climbed high bluffs overlooking the river, where pines grew amid lichen fields. The weather was sunny with highs in the upper sixties, simply a great day to be hiking the Econfina. I laughed at the thought of hundreds of thousands of spring breakers currently mobbing greater Panama City, which lay but forty miles to the south. Here I was all alone in the beauty of blooming azaleas and a few mountain laurels, which were trying their best to open before March was out. More sights were ahead, in the form of massive clear first magnitude springs boiling up from the river's edge. First magnitude springs are those that emit in excess of a hundred cubic feet per second, which is one hellacious fountain.

The bluffs formed limestone walls that dropped fifty feet to the water's edge. From this vantage, I could peer down into the Econfina river bottom and see river-created flow patterns. Different tones of tan showed depth as the water ran over sandy bottoms and around submerged logs. On the bluffs, water had created other patterns as it flowed from land to river. The FT passed still more bluffs, then discreetly turned away from the Econfina River, without fanfare or celebration. It kept going along a high bluff into open woods on a track that resembled a sandtrap in a forgotten par nine golf course. The trail then entered sand pine woods, with the red-bronze needles covering the ground, making the soil so acidic that only sparkleberry bushes dared grow here. The sun lit the sparkleberry leaves, giving them a bright green glow against the brown-trunked sand pines with their dark green needles.

I dropped to Little Porter Pond and made camp under an oak, near the water. My feet were glad for a break from the pounding. I spent the balance of the sunny afternoon resting. The FT was leaving the

One feeder branch offered a waterfall.

forest again tomorrow, with more road walking ahead. The trail had once continued through wooded St. Joe paper lands, but they were developing the property and thus the FT was routed back onto State Road 20. This was just a temporary setback in the evolution of the Florida Trail, much as we have setbacks in our lives, from which we not only recover but move on to bigger and better things.

I retired by the fire under starry skies, only to be awakened by drops of rain pelting on the sleeping bag, making a sort of muddled thud, as my head was mostly inside the bag except for a breathing hole near my mouth. The weather forecast had called for rain coming after dawn, but apparently the rain didn't get the message. Setting up a working shelter in the dark from a dead sleep can be challenging, but I was all too familiar with this situation. My camping buddies know that despite evidence to the contrary, including black clouds and a bleak forecast, I am still likely to say, "It's not gonna rain." Whereupon I am faced with this very situation. Luckily while gathering firewood I had scouted the area, looking for a potential tarp spot in case it rained. I covered my bedding with the plastic sleeping pad, ran over to a stand of sand pines, and rigged up the poncho/tarp to withstand some precipitation. Then I gathered my belongings and stuffed them under the tiny tarp, eking out a space to bed down.

I ran back to see if anything had been left on the ground, then returned to sleep until about at 4:00 a.m. Rain still fell. I donned my jacket and made a fire for coffee. Taking some toilet paper and semidry needles and a few twigs from under the tarp over to the fire ring, I flipped over the top layer of burned wood, revealing dry coals. I put the paper and twigs over the dry coals and lit the pile, leaning over the tiny fire as it got started, shielding it from rain, and inhaling smoke in the process. The fire did well and I threw on some wood I had already gathered for the morning, then boiled some water, made coffee, and huddled under to the tarp to drink it. The light of the fire glowed through the thin shelter. I repeated the performance for two cups of coffee and two hot chocolates, hoping the rain would end as I waited for dawn.

If you ever wondered about the downside of hiking, this is it. Breaking camp in the rain, in the dark, ain't no fun at all. But I packed the pack under the tiny shelter, then quickly took down the tarp, unstrung the string used to tie it to limbs, and threw the green plastic shelter over me and the pack, which now morphed from tarp to poncho. I took off up the hill, away from the lake, into a passel of sand pines as the rain pelted the dawn.

The rain intensified. I felt like the protagonist in a bad video game called Battle for the Morning. The trail opened into young low woods, revealing the contour of the land. Before me were green hills—dips and swales that could have been Kentucky. I reached State Road 20 two miles from camp and began an extensive road walk. The chill air was inviting, but the blasts from oncoming trucks were not. In places a sand track ran parallel to the road, letting me get away from the cars. If road walking with a pack isn't humiliating enough, getting sprayed by cars certainly is. After a couple of hours, the rain tapered off, leaving a fog. Supposedly, the Florida Trail Association had a newly acquired tract of land ending this road walk for future thru-hikers. Vast tree farms of pine bordered most of the road.

Cars remained my noisy companions as I plowed west along the road. The sun even came out that afternoon, as I trekked into Bruce, a one-convenience-store intersection of a town. My legs and willpower had taken me twenty-four miles, and I went into the store for a little supper and a gallon of water, ready to make another hobo camp. The houses of the town didn't extend far past the convenience store, and I followed a woods track off SR 20 into some pines. The old road ended after a hundred yards and had become a dumping ground. Vines and pine needles covered an old washer, some roofing, and other assorted stuff I didn't care to explore. At that point I didn't care to find a better spot, either. I was whipped, and the sun was lowering. This hobo retired not long after dark, with the whirring cars still my companions, as they had been all that day.

20

Bedding Down

I was back on the road at dawn, breaking camp by firelight and head-lamp, trying to make the most of the chilly morning and giving my-self ample time to make the nineteen miles to the foot trail that the Florida Trail became once it reached the friendly confines of Eglin Air Force Base. I had a lot of roadside foot-pounding to do before that point. The town of Freeport was nine miles away. I made the cold march.

This second long road walk brought out the worst in me. I watched passersby in their cars, staring at me in what seemed an utterly blank manner. Even the cows were more curious. I quit looking back, or waving, or anything. I wanted to give them some hand signals we won't mention, especially the ones stuffing their faces behind the wheel as they drove. I wanted to yell, "Why, fat slob, are you staring at someone who is actually getting some exercise? You are looking at a person who has a car, owns a house, and is self-employed at a job he loves!"

I gave them miserable lives, though I didn't know their names or where they lived, or what their interests were. I looked at the cover and decided what was inside the book. My mind would wander away from the Starers, as I began to call them, perhaps to glance at a house by the road and wonder why its occupants chose to display in the front yard every car they had ever owned, whether it ran or not. Or wonder if there was an ordinance limiting how many deer, ducks, and other statuettes could be put in front of one home. Or wonder why one homeowner could keep such an immaculate yard while the neighbor lived in such a mess. What was the difference between them?

Inevitably, I also thought about how the pack on my back weighed too much and what was going out at the next place where I could discard it. I might look down and count beer bottles along the road in a fifteen-minute period. Or wonder how a credit card, still current, ended up on the side of the road (I broke it in half). Such were the musings of a hiker doing a little road walking on the Florida Trail.

I arrived in Freeport, a future ex-country town, about to explode. Land was for sale everywhere, and new developments with names like "Windswept" were going up. That's Florida for you, growing, growing, growing. Instead of discarding things, however, I pulled into Kelley's Supervalu grocery (soon to be supplanted by a chain grocery, I expect) and loaded up. A teen offered to push my groceries out, but I told him I had no car to which to take them. He looked puzzled. Nobody walks to the grocery store any more, except perhaps in New York City. The wind nearly blew me down as I walked out of the store and pushed my shopping cart to a bench by the storefront to load the groceries into the pack. I should just put my pack in the cart and push it, I thought.

The morning cold was compounded by a strong north wind, and I donned a jacket for the final road march, turning north onto US Highway 331. A mass exodus of out of state cars was heading north, too. It was Friday and many vacationers were heading home from the beaches of Panama City. With heavy pack and heavier legs, weary of road marching, I began to call this road the "Motorway of Misery," for all its bad vibes. The vacationers had had their fun and spent their money and were looking at a boring drive, returning to staid lives. They would be getting a credit card bill in the mail, in about a month, for the fun they'd already had in Florida. At least the past week had been warm for them.

Tracing an open power line right-of-way that ran parallel to the road made my walk much easier, despite my forgetting to get water in Freeport. Boy, was I thirsty. The vacationers probably had a few drinks left in their coolers, I thought. I visualized running out to the road and flagging one down to say, "Excuse me, do you have cool beverage?" Pride wouldn't let me, of course. Later, a clear stream cut under the power line, and my thirst was sated, pride intact. At last, after nine more miles of road warrioring, the FT turned into the woods of the huge Eglin AFB. The land that harbored Eglin was originally established as the Choctawhatchee National Forest in 1908 and was taken over by the Air Force in 1940. Some of it had been used as a bombing range, but mostly it was left intact with a modicum of forest management, and it is thus one of the great undisturbed forests in the state.

I reveled in the wind whooshing through the pines, the sun heating up needle fragrance from the ground, rather than the roar of a truck followed by the stench of uncombusted diesel. The clear blue skies and frontal passage gave the hilly forest a vibrant look, as opposed to the dark, misty washed-out terrain of the day before. The sloped land featured an abundance of pine, turkey oaks on its sandiest hills, grass, and clumps of palmetto and yaupon holly growing where it best suited them. The woodland mosaic—exactly where something grows and something else doesn't—had general patterns, but I often couldn't discern why what grew where. It just was.

Spring steepheads emerged from gaps in the high hills, pouring swift clear water over sandy bottoms, which cut ever deeper beneath the shade of titi, sparkleberry, magnolia, and beech. The streams tumbled over fallen logs, splashing noisily down to the lowest reaches of land, places like Alaqua Creek, which formed true bottomland; places where cypress was king. Despite the inspiring beauty, my energy was flagging during the last two miles to Eglin Portal campsite, located near a confluence of unnamed streams. After dropping the supply-laden pack, I walked on air.

The chill wind blew strongly all afternoon, so I rested in the sunshine until it went behind the trees, and I made a fire using an abundance of turkey oak, which makes a hot, slow-burning, and relatively smokeless fire. The wind died at dark. Streams serenaded me in the distance. The resonance, the music of moving water, is one of the most soothing sounds in nature, a treat by which to sleep. I retired close to the fire on this 30-degree night and was overjoyed to see the dawn as I peered with one eye from my refuge. The upside of the cold snap was the utter lack of mosquitoes; I slept in the open, as usual when the skeeters weren't an issue.

The cold got me moving quickly, although it would be an easy day of only eight miles. This was the first short day I'd had in a while, and my lower body was feeling the effects of forty-seven miles in the past two days. The trail alternated between shady cold ravines where the pretty streams ran and the pine-dominated uplands, open to the warming sun. Holly grew in surplus on the slopes and was the predominant understory tree on the hillsides between the tangled creek bottoms and the pine crests. I came to sandy Blount Creek, a larger stream, transparent, with a sand bottom and bordered by mountain laurel bushes, which were displaying their pink and white blooms. Smooth-barked beech trees spotted with patches of moss contrasted with magnolia leaves reflecting the glint of the morning sun.

The FT then climbed a hill or two before reaching the wide bottomland of big Alaqua Creek, where cane formed reedy regiments. A live tree had fallen over Alaqua Creek, which was about twenty feet wide at this point. The trunk of the tree didn't make it all the way, so someone had nailed to its limbs a pair of boards that did extend to the opposite bank. They made up the creek bridge now. I gingerly walked the first plank, and made it fine, then made it across the second plank to the second limb. Next I had to step over a wire strung alongside, presumably to help provide balance, though I found it unhelpful. I reached the main trunk and tightroped across the Alaqua. I have crossed many a log in my hiking days and believe most of the challenge is in your mind. If you expect to make it, then you usually do. Those who fall didn't think they could or get 90 percent of the way across and then lose concentration and take a tip. You aren't across until you are across. A life lesson is in there somewhere.

The tree bridge took me to a peninsula nearly encircled by Alaqua Creek. Here, you could see, the water simply ran over the peninsula during flood conditions, rather than going around the peninsula, as it did at normal flows. One day the creek would simply cut through the peninsula for good and leave behind an oxbow swamp where it had once flowed. Then the makeshift bridge would be useless.

Flame azaleas, named for their fierce orange color, grew in this bottom, along with cypress. Periodic high water had carved undulations in the land, depositing debris against trees, and leaving the living trees to bend downstream after the waters receded and the debris to rot back to the earth. High water also replenished and refilled the overflow oxbow swamps carved by past waters.

The FT popped back out to the "high country," which was warming by now. I reveled in the weather and scenery and craved more. When you are taking an 1,100-mile walk, there are up times like this, and down times, times when you wish the trip was through or you wish you were somewhere else; I was beginning to realize the adventure would be ending, for better or worse.

I reached Alaqua Camp on Hellfire Creek well before noon. I was ready to languish away the day, enjoying the sights and sounds of nature as opposed to the road walk scenes, which still wore on my mind and body. I relaxed in the warming spring sun, reflecting on the trip. I now had less than a hundred miles to hike. I thought ahead too, making posthike plans, but I didn't stray too far from the moment, for this moment would only happen once. Always it is now, and now was where I wanted to be. Alaqua Camp was a great place, a well-groomed camp in level sand pines, with a picnic table for convenience and a metal fire ring.

Another day of solitude. I was surprised not to see other hikers, as it was an ideal Saturday. All day I was prepared to hear voices, other backpackers rolling into camp, but I saw no other human being. The 60-degree day became a cold night, and once again I had to compensate for my underinsulated bag. I gathered turkey oak wood, along with some sand pine, and stacked it all by the fire ring, ready to throw on during the night.

The next morning was even colder, but at least I had a fire already going from my night feedings. The FT kept north, rolling over sand hills and cutting through dense swamp hardwood thickets, which covered only the lowermost part of the valley. The hills warmed me up and were at times steep enough to employ switchbacks. Switchbacks are a method used to surmount hills gradually, without going straight up or down, making a less erosive trail. The path is routed at an angle up a hill, gaining elevation moderately, then making an abrupt turn or switchback in the other direction, still angling upward, and so on to the high point you would have reached by climbing straight up the said hill.

The FT then turned west and began to parallel Interstate 10. The interstate noise detracted somewhat from this scenic and hilly land. As an affirmation of scenic pleasures, though, I came upon a patch of wildflowers in the margin where the thickets of Bull Creek met open sand hills. The stream/hill pattern continued all the way to Red Deer campsite on that seventeen-mile day.

Along the way I had run into a camouflaged turkey hunter. He had seen a hiker or two pass this way during his hunting trips on Eglin. We both thought the air force base offered some of Florida's finest scenery, scenery unknown to most Sunshine State residents. Red Deer campsite was attractive, a flat spot on a piney hill, if was a little too close to I-10. Red Deer had the reality of isolation, even if thousands were motoring nearby, oblivious to the Florida Trail and a lone backpacker hearing their passage. I thought about how the day's seventeen miles had been easier, in a way, than the previous day's eight miles. I'd had the mindset of expecting to go seventeen miles, had known it would take much of the day, and wasn't anxious about it; the day before, with the short miles, I continually expected to be at the campsite quickly and wanted to be there before I was there.

I'd made lunch near Cowpen Branch. The air was still cold, as I could tell by the Peanut Butter Index. When you have peanut butter, you scarcely need a thermometer. If you open the jar and can't dig in with your spoon, then it's cold. If the paste has the consistency of a milkshake, you know it's warm. The night was colder yet, and the skies were clear. I looked up and saw Orion, the Archer, again. He'd been following me since South Florida, fading out when the moon was waxing, but always tailing.

I began making up my bed, planning to wear lots of clothes in the sleeping bag. Irrationally, I surmised that since it was officially spring, the cold snap would ease; but it hung tough. Wearing all my clothes to bed left me little with which to make a pillow. I am known for stacking anything I can to get my head high, and compadres have often made fun of the structures upon which I lay my head. Since it wasn't going to rain and the skeeters were nonexistent, I filled my sleeping bag stuff sack with the poncho/tarp and the mosquito netting. I looked around for more and put in the roll of toilet paper to give the rig a little more height, then lay down. No go. With the headlamp I rummaged through the pack and added a bandana to the stuff sack. Then I slid in the *Florida Trail Companion Guide*. The result was better, but my neck was still a little crooked. I decided to put the pack itself under the filled stuff sack. Yes! A good piece of backpacking equipment is one that serves at least two purposes.

Finally I lay down in comfort. That was when I felt the slope of the land beside the fire ring. I am accustomed to sleeping on less than level land in the mountains, but this was too much. I had to hang on to the sleeping pad to keep from rolling over. Dang! Further measures were required. Again I fired up the headlamp, disrupting my perfectly arranged pillow and sleeping bag so as to pad the setup with some bunches of needles, collectively called pine straw. Trip by trip I gathered and moved the pine straw to create a level sleeping area by the fire. Suddenly my sleeping area went from subpar to superb, although sleeping on pine straw by a fire ain't too bright. But when I placed the sleeping pad and bag and pillow in their appropriate positions and created a backpacker's bed, I did sleep like a king with the extra padding, insulation, and pillow that were all just right. Goldilocks and the Three Bears would have been proud of me.

I left Red Deer campsite well rested and ready to go. Brisk mornings like this meant a runny nose, cold fingers, and numb ears, but once I got going the hiking was invigorating. I headed west, crossing Gum Creek, which was choked with bay, cane, and titi as well as gum, a deciduous swamp tree also known as tupelo. The morning chill hung in the thick bottoms, whereas on the sand hills the air was warming. Titi Creek flowed yellow and was part of the greater Yellow River drainage. The hills above Titi Creek were the highest I had seen on the entire hike. The well-maintained trail continued across lightly forested sand hills, then into creek bottom jungle. The path was staying as close to Eglin's outer perimeter as possible, keeping the interior open for bombing practice. Florida Trail Association members call this "The Land of Was That Thunder?" referring to the Air Force training exercises.

Silver Creek was not silver, but it was see-through and open to the sky overhead. Underwater grasses waved in the current as water pushed down the valley over a waffled sandy bottom. I had to drink some of that. Leaning down from the footbridge that spanned the stream and filling the water bottle, I turned the bottle up like a man dying of thirst, water dribbling from the corners of my mouth onto my shirt.

Near my destination, Pearl Creek, the hills gave way to continuous bottomland, and the trail resorted to following an old raised road-bed above wetland before reaching the Pearl campsite, in pine-oak woods. By now the brilliant sun had completely warmed the day and I relaxed sans shirt, shoes, and socks. I went over to Pearl Creek. It was aquarium clear. I walked onto a log to get water. The sun sliced through a break in the canopied titi, illuminating the sand bottom of the creek, where small turtles lay still, unaware of a large potential predator above them. Minnows darted from the slack water behind a submerged log, inspecting passing debris for edibility.

I returned to camp, reveling in the warm day. Suddenly I heard steps pattering across the dry leaves, getting louder. I looked up, and a tan coyote sauntered right toward me. It stopped in its tracks but twenty feet distant, inventorying the suddenly unpleasant situation, then reversed course at high speed. That's the way it happens, seeing wildlife. More often that not you have to let it come to you, for when you search for it, your very movement, often loud and clumsy, is heard by critters long before they come within sight, and they skitter away. That's why deer, duck, and turkey hunters silently plant themselves in stands or blinds and let the creatures come to them.

The backpack cupboard was getting thin again. I had noodle fare that evening, without even the added bulk of the instant mashed potatoes. I ate out of my black cooking pot, as usual, scraping every last noodle piece from the bottom. That was all I had to eat, so I ate it all. The *scrape, scrape, scrape* of spoon on pot had become the sound of nonfulfillment, the sound of hunger, the sound of that's all there was and you better save anything else you have because you are going to be hungry tomorrow, too.

Tomorrow became today and I walked the last mile through Eglin. It had exceeded my high expectations. But now it was time to proceed on, since all I had left for the morning was hot chocolate and coffee. I was hungry. There was a grocery store in nearby Crestview. The trail turned north at State Road 85 and headed into Crestview, the seat of exponentially growing Okaloosa County. This road walk would be eliminated in the next few years, as the FT was routed west along the Yellow River valley, yet farther west through Eglin. I was glad for future hikers, but for me the reality was another road walk. The cars were as noisy as ever and the stares as blank, but I didn't care, as this was the final road walk.

I reloaded at the local Publix grocery store, unfazed even by the whole grocery buying affair at this point. Out front I "edited" my pack, removing what I could, getting rid of as much extraneous packaging as possible, then cramming everything back, the proceedings on display for all the shoppers entering and exiting the store. As invariably happened in such public situations, curiosity overcame shyness and someone drifted over to quiz me. A woman sitting on a bench smoking a long cigarette overheard my desire to pass through town and kept interjecting with bus schedules for Crestview. The man quizzing me ignored the woman, seemingly familiar with her, while I tried to explain that I was *hiking* the Florida Trail and therefore not interested in taking a bus. Things degenerated from there, all parties having barely related conversations. The man, a retired Yankee from New York, seemed to be killing time and might have let this go on forever, but the day was heating and I had miles to go. I put on my pack and excused myself, bidding them farewell. I thought about the woman, with oversized white sweatpants and a purple sweatshirt disguising her ultrathin frame, her face a skeletal outline, jaw flapping nonstop. I could see her rambling all over town on the Crestview bus system, driving the bus drivers crazy.

I walked on into the center of town. A guy yelled at me from a roof, "Where ya goin', the Blackwater?" I hollered back that I was. The roofer stopped working and walked down the slope to the roof's edge. He was referring to the Blackwater River State Forest and told me he ran a van shuttle for a canoe livery there in the summer. By this time the whole roofing crew had stopped, and the head honcho, standing on the ground, offered me a drink from their water cooler. I filled my bottle while the head honcho—who didn't look especially authoritative in his white T-shirt, cut-off blue jeans, and work boots—explained they were a roofing company of brothers and one cousin. They were truly interested in the hike (and perhaps looking for a break from roofing), so I showed them the contents of my pack, what I ate, the clothes and shelter I carried, and my solar-powered writing setup.

I mentioned that I had been visiting the area for fifteen years, canoeing around Crestview, and I couldn't believe the changes and how the place had transformed from sleeping inland Panhandle town to bustling Everywhereville. The head honcho agreed, mentioning how all the locals at the beaches to the south, namely at Fort Walton Beach, had sold out and moved here and that Air Force personnel were filling up the rest of the area. My nephew Derek, an airman twice stationed here, later confirmed the theory, adding that Crestview was dubbed "Crestucky" for the residents' rural bent. In my own estimation, Crestview will have lost all its southernness soon enough.

I left the roofers behind, with my own job to do: one last research stop for my guide to laundromats of the Florida Trail. I rate this one highly, mostly for its employees, two women who were nice as could be. They lived to the north, in Baker, where they said things were still quiet. Clean again, I turned west on US Highway 90 into a clouding sky, crossing the Yellow River, one of my favorite canoe camping streams. I grabbed a jug of water in Milligan, then walked a few miles and made another hobo camp. The hilltop woods were quite pleasant on a cloudy day.

The tables had turned. I was now counting down the miles instead of counting them up. You aren't there until you are there, but there was a perfunctory aspect to ending at the end point. Nevertheless I went full steam ahead, leaving the hobo camp at dawn and keeping west on US 90, passing occasional houses. Every house had a dog, and every dog had a way of acknowledging my presence, most often including continuous barking until I got out of sight.

It was still early when I made Holt, so I grabbed a little coffee at Bowman's, a country store. As the coffee was brewing I started a conversation with another man waiting for the pot to fill, and we adjourned outside to a wooden bench. Hugh Adams was thirty years my elder, with a full head of white hair and plenty of stories about Holt, a one-stop town built around the railroad. We were looking across the street at the now defunct school he had once attended. I asked him about the railroad behind us as I chewed on a ham biscuit. He stuck his thumbs into his overalls and told how he used to ride the train to Crestview on a Saturday with enough money for a ticket to the movies and some snacks, returning that same day on the evening train. No one rode the train any more. It was all freight. I asked what he did nowadays and he said, "Whittle." He walked over to his truck and gave me a palm-sized cedar carving, after signing it, "Hugh Adams, Holt, Fl." He said since it was cedar it wouldn't weigh my pack down too much. I thanked him for the souvenir and walked on, leaving another new friend behind. It's a way of life for a traveler.

21

Take Note of That

The last part of the last road walk led down US Highway 90 from Holt to Harold. Harold had a store, too, and was even smaller than Holt. As mentioned, future FT hikers will not have to bother with this part along US 90—they will still be in Eglin AFB, south of here, across the Yellow River. Everything in time.

Harold was also the last decision point for FT thru-hikers. I could hang a right and turn north to terminate at the Alabama state line, or I could continue west and south to end at Fort Pickens in Gulf Islands National Seashore. The seashore route sounded good, but in reality it entailed more road walking, and then I would enter the spring break zone at its zenith, with nowhere to camp. Not even a hobo could find a place to lay his head, unless perhaps in some boxes behind a convenience store. The final part traveled a Gulf sand beach to end near the Fort Pickens campground, which was still closed following hurricane damage. When the alternative was to hike through Florida's largest state forest of 200,000 acres in the midst of woods and waterways that I considered among the best in the state, camping wherever I pleased, there was not much doubt about the decision. Ironically, on numerous trips to Fort Pickens, I had seen the oceanside terminus of the FT and had always visualized ending there.

Ambling up Deaton Bridge Road, fixing to enter the state forest, I ran into a Florida Trail crew. First off, the crew—consisting of two retired men—evinced disbelief that they were actually seeing a thru-hiker. In all their days of working on trails, I was the first they had seen. I told them I appreciated their hard work, and one of them told me I would likely be the last person to hike along Deaton Bridge

Road. They were putting the finishing touches on a new FT segment that routed hikers off the road. Progress. These two men represented the can-do spirit of the Florida Trail, literally turning an idea hatched in the 1960s into a reality for the new millennium. I thanked them for their work.

At that juncture, up came the Blackwater River State Park manager, Bob Barlow. The park adjoined the state forest, and Bob was helping manage a prescribed burn. He had been working for the Florida state parks for nearly three decades. I was showing the trail crew my writing setup when some supplies fell out of my pack. I reloaded the whole affair and headed on, after asking Bob for a trail map of the Blackwater; I had none, because my original plan had been to end the hike at the national seashore. Bob said he would stop at the office and leave a map for me on a fence a few miles up the trail.

I proceeded on, reaching the Blackwater River. I stopped in a secluded spot and jumped in, rinsing off the dirt and road grime, then hid while drying. After donning my duds I was on my way north again, into a now sunny day. The trail rolled over hills of pine divided by low titi thickets, through which murmured small streams. Long boardwalks in the thickets made them much easier to traverse than the sloppy thickets back in the Apalachicola National Forest.

I came to the wire fence where Bob had left the map. Something else hung on the wire. I came closer. Bob had also left me a cigar, a big fat really good cigar! He must have seen the junk cigars that had fallen out of my pack while we were talking and figured I was due for a good one to celebrate the completion of the Florida Trail. What a man.

Two quick miles brought me to Alligator Creek, an unlikely looking spot for alligators. The fast-moving stream cut a ravine in the hills, shaded by Atlantic white cedar and forming a dark cool line in the open pine hills. A wooden bridge spanned the breezy ravine. A little flat near it became camp. I couldn't wait until the end of the trail to fire up the stogie, instead puffing it on the bank of Alligator Creek, watching the sun descend between the nearby pines. It was a celebration nonetheless. The end was imminent. Just then I heard two men talking on the trail ahead. One had a foreign accent, the other a southern accent.

At this point I was sitting in the middle of the trail. They couldn't miss me, and I couldn't miss them. "To hell with it," I said and didn't move but just sat, smoking the cigar. The two stopped. They were wearing full backpacks. The southerner, about fifty with a gray beard, wore a long-sleeved shirt over his ample midsection. He asked my name. He said he'd heard of me, from a hiking book I'd written. Then I quizzed them, and the foreign fellow turned out to be Ronnie, who had been hiking the Florida Trail ahead of me. I'd seen his postings at trail registers along the way. He had always ended his postings "Ronnie (from Israel)"; like that, in parentheses. These two had met on a long distance hike of the Pacific Crest Trail and were having a reunion of sorts.

Ronnie (from Israel) had glasses that magnified his eyeballs, and he sported a bushy, curly beard and a French Foreign Legion hat with a skirt covering his neck and ears. A black long-sleeved shirt covered his arms, and he wore short pants. On his hands were gloves, for use with his trekking poles. On the whole, the thirty-year-old painted a funny picture. But he had walked the walk in the style that worked for him, completing his FT thru-hike. He'd already completed other long distance hikes before this, including the Appalachian Trail. Now they were backtracking to the southerner's car, to go and eat some real food.

They bickered and sniped at each other like an old married couple, half in fun, half trying to get their point across, continually interrupting each other. I could hardly keep up with them. They were considering whether to camp with me or go and get some meat. Ronnie kept saying, "I crave meat." Then he'd say, "But I want to talk about the Florida Trail with another thru- hiker." The southerner was trying to appease him, but that is hard to do with someone changing his mind from moment to moment. The meat won the day, although the southerner lamented how much weight he had gained since his long distance hike of the Pacific Crest Trail. He said, "I can't stop eating like I'm on the trail. I've gained forty pounds." I took note of that.

White dogwoods lit up the foggy morning.

It was about dark by the time they left, still sniping back and forth as they crossed Alligator Creek. I kept replaying the wacky encounter in my head while lying in the sleeping bag that night, Alligator Creek gurgling in the background. You can't make up stuff like that. I was glad to have met another thru-hiker, even though he had already finished.

The next day was short. I was going only four miles. The trail wound among cedars, magnolias, and tall bushes by the sandy banks of Juniper Creek. The FT along Juniper Creek showed effects of Hurricane Ivan, with an unbelievable number of fallen trees. Atlantic white cedars had fallen on top of one another like players in a rugby scrum. Backpackers had to twist through the sawn passages. The forest would take years to recover. Clearing the passage had been hard work. Mountain laurel bloomed in places. In the hills, where the trail worked away from the creek, white dogwoods lit up the foggy morning.

I reached a trail shelter near a bluff overlooking Juniper Creek. The shelter offered shade and the bluff provided a good view of Juniper Creek below, where I could get water and cool off when the furnace started heating up. It was a fine place to camp, among the best on the trail. I whiled away the day, knowing this would be the last lazy day for the foreseeable future. Nary a soul came by; yet another day in Florida when I didn't see anyone else, despite road access to the trail not much more than a mile distant. It was a weekday, however, and the warriors were at work, counting the minutes until Friday at 5:00 p.m., leaving the woods to me. Though the hours daylight were longer now. I went to bed shortly after dark, as the bulb on the headlamp was getting dim. Also, I wanted to get an early jump the next morning, as I was looking at a day of more than twenty miles.

I left camp before light, navigating the trail with the weak lamp. I ambled down the trail onto a sandbar on Juniper Creek. The white sand reflected what light drifted from the heavens, but I couldn't find where the trail left the sandbar. After scouting in circles for fifteen minutes, I decided to backtrack to the shelter and start again. This time I stayed with the orange blazes, which never went to the sandbar at all. I had followed a spur trail created by hikers wanting to check out the creek. So much for the early start.

Dawn came and the world opened before me. The number of blooming dogwoods was stunning. They were puffy clouds of white lighting the pine woods. Birds were having chirping contests. The trail, blocked with dewy spider webs, angled east as I passed through pine stands, timber harvests, and a recent burn where regenerating bracken ferns formed a green carpet over the blackened ground. The forest floor was wet from fog, but the rising sun took care of that.

On and on I went, crossing over to the east bank of the Blackwater River on a road bridge. I was in great hiking shape now, and the miles just melted away. The Florida Trail was tracing the Jackson Red Ground Trail, which followed the route of Andrew Jackson as he headed south into what was then New Spain during the early Seminole Wars. The path climbed a high ridge where pine trees formed a dispersed forest. The needle-covered trail often skirted the sides of this ridge and adjoining hills, around which seepage slopes formed dense grassy patches from which rose pitcher plants, red, green, and white. They preferred these moist margins, as did maple and bay trees. By afternoon the Florida Trail turned west, leaving the high pines for the Blackwater River, crossing feeder creeks and more seepage slopes full of pitcher plants. Azaleas bloomed nearby. Finally, the trail reached the river, and a small flat on a bluff under some sparkleberry bushes.

I had camped here before and knew my destination before I left the shelter that morning. My hiking buddy John Cox and I had executed a six-day trip in the Blackwater. We had hiked the Florida Trail from the Blackwater River up to Kennedy Bridge and Hurricane Lake Campground, where I had left my Jeep. We then unloaded my canoe off the Jeep and floated back down the Blackwater River to our point of origin. On the hike up we had done the same long walk from the shelter to this point. John had gotten his ass kicked and exemplified the Five-Foot Radius Theory of Camping—you don't move more than five feet from where you drop your pack. (This is a variation on the Twenty-Foot Theory illustrated by my earlier companion Jeff in the scrubby sea of the Ocala National Forest weeks before.) Shortly after arriving, John climbed into his sleeping bag while I cooked some hot dogs. He was so tired that he ate his hot dogs lying on his back, still in the bag, shoveling them in one by one. Have you ever tried to eat while lying on your back in a sleeping bag? It's harder than it sounds. To do this he ate dry dogs, just the meat and the bun, no fixin's. He was whipped.

My dinner this time wasn't much better than dry dogs—the final noodling. The continuous exercise and limited fare had left me fifteen pounds lighter, despite the fact that I take outdoor quests for a living. The weight loss surprised me. I had expected to drop a few pounds but not fifteen. Perhaps my next book should be called *The 1,100 Miles of Noodles Diet Handbook*. How do you think it will do against the South Beach Diet? It was hard falling asleep on this final night on the trail. I was excited about completing the hike, and life beyond the

Florida Trail was looming larger; this wasn't a bad thing, just something that loomed.

I heard the first bird chirp on the last morning on the Florida Trail while leaving the little sparkleberry camp by the river. The trail led straight into a fresh burn. Black, dry soot crunched beneath my shoes, and the odor of burnt pine rose strong into the warm, humid morn. No smoke, though. The trail crossed a forest road that delineated the burn area and I was soon back on the edge of the Blackwater River, in incredible tangles of fallen limbs and trees, also testimony to Ivan. The trail had been rerouted in several places to get beyond tree piles that amazed me when I considered the force needed to put them in their fallen positions. Respect the power of a hurricane.

The trail popped out at Kennedy Bridge and circled around the aptly named Hurricane Lake. It was a Saturday morning and campers were having a ball, fishing, cooking up fine-smelling breakfasts, kids hollering, all good innocent fun. I crossed the grass-covered earthen dam of the lake and rambled through hills, turning north again toward Alabama. The hills steepened and clear creeks sliced between them, delivering tasty water. I pressed on, now excited to see what the end looked like. I had visualized all sorts of things—a pair of signs marking the respective state borders, a "You Made It!" banner, or simply the last orange blaze ending at some indefinable boundary of the state forest.

A deer dashed from a ravine, crossing my path. It was just another day for one of nature's beasts, knowing no deadlines, dates, or weekends. This was my last day out with them and I stood perched on the cusp of such time constraints.

Along the way I passed the crescendo of pitcher plant colonies. I had to stop and take a picture, end of the trail or no. Here, the green "pitchers" were tipped in white, over which hung maroon flowers so deeply colored as to seem fake. Nature never quits on the Florida Trail. Ahead, the trail dipped and I could see some signage. This was it! Sure enough, a kiosk showed details of the Florida Trail and another trail, heading into Alabama.

Pitcher plants tipped in white were overhung by maroon flowers so deeply colored as to seem fake.

I pulled up to the sign, located in piney woods, took a deep breath, and sat on a bench after shedding the pack. Was I expecting an epiphany? Or to be overwhelmed and have a trailside apoplectic fit upon finishing the FT? Or for a beam of light to shine down from on high, illuminating me physically and mentally, showing me the answers to life? No. Were you? Sorry if you were, but in long distance hiking—and long distance living, also known as the course of our lives—*it really is the journey that matters, not the destination.*

I thought back on the highs and lows, the sights seen, friends made, aches, pains, joys, and simply the passage of time. I hadn't waited for the end to experience and absorb the Florida Trail; it had been an adventure all the way. If you are always looking ahead to when you finish this or that, so that then you will be happy and will be equipped with knowledge to navigate life, then you may be waiting for something that won't happen. It just doesn't bear out. Learning life's lessons on a daily basis, applying them, with an appetite for learning more, serves best. Be in the moment.

For the past seventy-eight days I lived the moments that were the Florida Trail. Was I a changed man after that? Where you end up in life depends on where you start. I had had an idea of what the hike would be like, and living in the outdoors wasn't new to me. The biggest surprise was being more awestruck by the beauty than I had expected. I'd already seen a lot of the real natural Florida, but the hike extended my sense of the depth and breadth of scenic finery that the Sunshine State offers. Was I better off for it? Absolutely. To see the wild splendor from the Everglades to the St. Johns to the western end of the Panhandle, to experience the mosaic of landscapes that covers this swath of the United States, was a reaffirmation of how lucky we are to live in such a stunning country. And the conception, construction, and eventual completion of the Florida Trail demonstrate American can-do spirit and determination. To follow the orange blazes was an honor and a monument to all those who had made the Florida Trail a reality.

Along the way, I had wondered what the actual moment of completion would feel like. From the first step I had expected to finish the trail, so completing it was not a surprise but a satisfaction, joy and gratefulness intermingled into one great rush.

A register was at the kiosk. I signed it, indicating my days of start and finish, with a few other comments. I savored the moment for just a moment, then hoisted on my pack for the last time and began to figure out how to get to the road where my nephew Derek was to pick me up.

Then I saw the orange blazes ahead.

I wasn't finished! I hurriedly walked on, tracing the same orange markers that I'd been following through the state. They led to a dirt road and the actual state line. Appropriately painted onto a pine tree was the last orange blaze. I had completed the Florida Trail. I raised a fist into the air and thanked God for giving me the strength to make it happen.

I left trail's end and followed a rough sand track west to reach Beaver Creek Road. The sand track came out exactly at the state line; I knew because the pavement suddenly got decrepit heading into Alabama. I sat in the shade sipping the last of the swamp water, hungrily waiting for Derek. I had cut the food supply to the edge, and the pack was empty.

Since Derek had been an Air Force man for more than fourteen years, he had learned timeliness and wasn't going to be late. I was an hour early. Hardly a car passed as the heat and humidity rose to numbers more like summer than early spring. I faced into Florida and watched a shiny purple souped-up Mustang rumbling up the road. I stood up. It had to be Derek. He is fond of fast, loud muscle cars. And it was. He hopped out, a man in great shape who could probably hike the FT if that were his bag. I threw my pack and dirty self into the immaculate car and we powered south through the Blackwater State Forest at speeds that mocked my hiker's pace.

We grabbed a drink then hit Interstate 10, blitzing east, catching up on family news and such. He had just gotten married. We stopped again to eat, and yes, I ate all I could at the all-you-can-eat buffet—which was a lot; I was paying no mind to the southerner's tale of gaining posthike weight. About 140 miles later, we stopped at an exit and met John and Barb Haapala, who were coming in my Jeep from the east, having driven it up from South Florida. I thanked my reliable nephew for the ride, then drove John and Barb back to Ocean Pond Campground, where they were staying. I would spend the night with them.

As I pointed the Jeep north toward Tennessee in the morning, abiding impressions chased one another through my mind, jostling for primacy. The snakes and alligators of which I'd been warned beforehand were way down the list. Instead I thought of noodles and laundromats, marshes, swamps, mosquitoes, and wet-shoe days—why would anyone want to be proceeding on through those? Because

My nephew Derek Molloy (right) retrieved me at the end of the trail, and my friend John Haapala reunited me with my car.

of the freedom and quiet beauty; the rich mix of natural landscapes; the close portrait of hurricane sculpting; the bursting exuberance of spring; and the pleasure of having all you can see entirely to yourself.

Florida Trail Quantified

Miles:	1,100
Days:	78
Average:	14 miles per day
Shortest Day:	3 miles
Longest Day:	26 miles
Zero Days (no hiking):	0

Best Long Trail Sections:

1. Big Cypress National Preserve
2. St. Marks National Wildlife Refuge
3. Apalachicola National Forest
4. Ocala National Forest
5. Blackwater River State Forest
6. Suwannee River

Best Shorter Trail Sections:

1. Econfina Creek of Washington County
2. Rice Creek Sanctuary
3. Hickory Hammock Wildlife Management Area
4. Three Lakes Wildlife Management Area
5. Tosohatchee State Preserve
6. Bull Creek Wildlife Management Area

Best Vistas:

1. Lake Okeechobee
2. Devils Mountain on Suwannee River
3. Kissimmee River Prairie
4. Seminole Section Dikes
5. Econfina Creek Bluffs

Best Trail Towns:

1. White Springs
2. Lake Butler
3. Blountstown
4. St. Marks
5. Moore Haven

Johnny Molloy is an outdoor writer based in Johnson City, Tennessee. A native Tennessean, he was born in Memphis and moved to Knoxville in 1980 to attend the University of Tennessee. It was in Knoxville that he developed his love of the natural world, which has since become the primary focus of his life.

It all started on a backpacking foray into the Great Smoky Mountains National Park. That first trip, though a disaster, unleashed an innate love of the outdoors that has led to his spending over a hundred nights in the wild per year over the past twenty-five years, backpacking and canoe camping throughout our country.

After graduating from the University of Tennessee with a degree in Economics, he continued to spend an ever-increasing amount of time in the natural places, becoming more skilled in a variety of environments. Friends enjoyed his adventure stories; one suggested he write a book. He pursued his friend's idea, and soon he had parlayed his love of the outdoors into an occupation.

The results of his efforts are more than thirty books, including hiking, camping, and paddling guidebooks, comprehensive guidebooks about specific areas, and outdoor adventure books. Molloy has also written numerous magazine articles and for Web sites as well. He continues to write and travel extensively to all corners of the United States, exploring a variety of outdoor pursuits. For the latest on Johnny, please visit www.johnnymolloy.com.